Brave, vigorous life
How a British public school prepared young men for
war, 1870-1914

David McDowell

LED BY **IWM**

For today's Fettes College Sixth Form,
whose next steps will be so very different from those
of their predecessors a century ago.

Contents

Acknowledgments

The material here is mostly taken from the school archives, and I would like to thank my colleague, Andrew Murray, for all of his help with my work there, and also Robert Philp, author of the original history of Fettes, *A Keen Wind Blows*.

The Headmaster, Michael Spens, the Bursar, Peter Worlledge, and Dawn Beaumont and Alastair Ross of the Old Fettesian Association were all generous in their support of the *Carrying On* project (the military history of Fettes from which much of the material in this book was taken).

Three Fettes chaplains – Brian McDowell, whose idea this was, David Campbell, who presided over the unveiling of the school's plaque in Ypres, and Tony Clark, who has continued to support Remembrance Week and Anzac Day in Chapel – are also owed thanks.

Rare are the events in modern history which cannot be connected to some former pupil's adventures, and my colleagues and students in the History Department at Fettes have kindly tolerated my tendency to pepper lessons with anecdotes on this theme.

Above all, I must thank Margaret Ann Loney, whose preferred period of history at university was the Scottish Enlightenment, for her forbearance as she has shared me with a strange collection of long-dead schoolboys.

Preface: The Photographs

Every autumn, the Fettes College history teachers give the third-formers photocopied pictures of their predecessors a hundred years ago. The rugby XV, the cricket team, the house sections of the cadet corps. The pupils are invited to look through school record books to see what became of them, and in many cases the results are what one would expect from a prestigious boarding-school like this – the manager of a large company, an eminent scientist or clergyman, the headmaster of a venerable grammar school, a senior civil servant, a stockbroker, a landowner, a colonial administrator.

In many cases, however, the record is cut short, with a terse line: 'killed at Loos, 27 Sept. 1915.' This applies to a third of the boys staring out sternly from the photo of the 1912 rugby team, and a third of the lads in kilts and glengarries gathered outside Moredun house with the cup they have won as most efficient cadets of 1913. A blue book, kept by the masters, is full of neatly-inscribed notes about the fates of the thousand pupils they had taught; a quarter of the names are underlined in red.

The third-formers use their laptops to find these individuals on the Commonwealth War Graves Commission website, and place them on big maps on the wall. Around two-fifths have no known graves; a similar proportion was aged twenty-five or under. The third-formers can now take part in Remembrance Day with the older pupils and with Old Fettesians, and make some sense of the annual ritual in chapel and around the school's impressive war memorial. They have seen their fallen brothers.

This book is intended to be the first in a series based on the research I originally carried out for *Carrying On: Fettes College, War and the World 1870-2010*. It treats Fettes College, the Edinburgh boarding school best known as the *alma mater* of the rather more modern British figures, James Bond and Tony Blair, as a microcosm of society – not a comprehensive one, to be sure, but one which was representative of many officers in the trenches. Through the experiences of the pupils of Fettes both during and after their schooldays, I hope to shed some light on what the average young man who led his troops over the top was thinking.

This first volume deals with life before the outbreak of war. Whilst some of the received wisdom has it that the young men of the clashing armies were innocents with no understanding of what they were doing, Fettesians and others had at least some awareness of the realities of war. This was developed formally through the training they received in the Officers' Training Corps, but also more widely in a school culture which emphasised endurance, courage and leadership. Moreover, the boys of Fettes, like those at other public schools, were regularly told about the realities of military life by former pupils serving in the armed forces.

The most important source document for this book is the school magazine, which recorded both events at the school, and the often exciting adventures of former pupils as they served the British Empire as soldiers or administrators. The *Fettesian* came out five or six times a year from the late 1870s, and is an extraordinary repository of stories and a great insight into contemporary attitudes. In addition, *Fifty Years of Fettes*, a collection of memories of former pupils put together just after the First World War, is a treasure-trove for the historian. The school also has copies of former pupils' memoirs and other books. Another invaluable document is the *Fettes Register*, which appeared regularly between the late nineteenth and mid-twentieth centuries, and recorded what former pupils had got up to.

This creates certain problems for the historian, however. The school was dependent on what information was available. The *Fettesian* reported that Percy D. Bailey's death 'occurred under very distressing circumstances' on 3 September 1898: he seems to have lost control of his bicycle on Brynfownog Hill en route from Bala to Lake Vyrnwy, and was killed. He had just left Cambridge, and was clearly popular. A correspondent noted mournfully that 'he is cut off in his early manhood, but he leaves the influence of a healthy, happy, earnest, thoroughly English life behind him.' Bailey's obituary, which included a report from the *Manchester Guardian*, merited two pages, whilst the unlucky G.H.O. Ziegler, who had died of yellow fever whilst working as an engineer on the railways of Costa Rica (of which he was 'a valued servant') only got a few lines.

Some entries in the *Register* are brief but intriguing. It has been possible to investigate a few, but others have been lost to history. All we know about A. Gibson is that he 'died in the interior of Peru in 1906', raising all manner of possibilities. On the other hand, although the entries for Robert Paterson Pattison and his brother Walter are brief, and they made no appearance in the *Fettesian*, this was not for lack of knowledge on the school's part. By the time the detailed study for the 1909 *Register* was carried out, the school – and everyone else in Edinburgh – knew exactly what they had been up to. Flamboyant entrepreneurs, they moved the family business from dairy to whisky and promoted themselves shamelessly from their grand premises in Leith and mansion in the Borders. They would ostentatiously miss scheduled trains so that they had to hire private ones, and are alleged to have trained five hundred parrots to recite their advertising slogans. However, their stock was grotesquely over-valued and they were desperately resorting to ruses such as selling their Irish whisky (valued at 11d. a gallon) as Glenlivet (8s. 6d. a gallon) in the hope that no-one would notice. Their company crashed spectacularly in 1898, taking nine others with it, with £743,000 owed to creditors. The brothers were imprisoned for fraud in 1901.[1] Another former pupil appears to have left the army under a cloud for some unbecoming but unspecified behaviour.

Needless to say, not a word of this ever appeared in a Fettes publication. Moreover, editors of the school magazine often complained about getting people to write for it (a sure-fire way of filling up space on the first two pages, especially when there didn't seem to be much going on in the world, was a ramblingly jocular editorial about how hard one's job could be). Fettes publications inevitably contain what 'the reticence of the editors or the nervousness of the censor' (as one former pupil put it) thought suitable to record. Fortunately, though, there is more than enough to give us a detailed picture of a world which was fatally wounded by the guns of August 1914, aspects of which seem scarcely credible today.

This is the story of how the educated upper middle classes of Victorian and Edwardian Britain prepared, not always consciously, for war. To read the pages of the school magazine in the decades before August 1914 is to be reminded of how important the military virtues were to the long-gone boys in those photographs, and their Victorian fathers. War was a regular and clearly visible spectre at the feast of cricket, classics and Christianity. This is not to say that a nineteen-year-old subaltern, ten months out of the Fettes sixth form and finding himself under fire for the first time, was bound to be wholly unperturbed by the experience. Thanks to the cultural hinterland he had acquired at school, however, he would not have been entirely surprised, he would have done his best to grin and bear it, and he might, at least in theory, have known how to lead others through the confusion. I hope that this book can give a wider audience an insight into that hinterland.

David McDowell
Fettes College, 2014

One of the old photographs investigated by the pupils; six of the boys in this pre-war 1ˢᵗ XV were killed in the Great War, including the captain, William Russell (centre), and five were wounded

The main building of Fettes College; the boys of Schoolhouse lived here until replaced by girls in the late twentieth century

1. The World of Fettes College

Sir William Fettes, who had made a fortune from supplying the army in the French wars and making questionable whisky, had no heir. William the younger had died whilst attempting the Grand Tour, and the evidence suggests that the old man did not hold his surviving relations in very high regard. He decided to bequeath the bulk of his fortune to good works, and set up a school for:

...young people whose parents have either died without leaving sufficient funds for that purpose, or who from innocent misfortune during their lives, are unable to give suitable education to their children.

Edinburgh had several such schools already, and after Sir William's death in 1836 the trustees of the Fettes Endowment for the Education, Maintenance and Outfit of Young People searched for ways to set up a different kind of institution. They found their model in England, where several of the great public schools were being transformed.

By the time they came to build the school in the 1860s, the funds (wisely invested) had swollen from the original £166,000 to almost half a million pounds – well over £34 million today. This enabled the Fettes trustees to build the most grandiose product of the imagination of Sir David Bryce, an architect whose style had become steadily more Gothic (some said eccentric) through the years. The boys of Fettes would study in a hybrid of Scottish baronial fortress, French Loire chateau, and Rosslyn Chapel. Sir David's vast confection might lack the austere good taste of the New Town, but it is an unmissable feature of the Edinburgh skyline. A newspaper report of June 1864, when the foundation-stone was laid, was enthusiastically reported that 'it will undoubtedly form one of the highest architectural embellishments of which the Scottish metropolis can boast.' Its vast windows, the despair of bursars faced with heating bills, were characteristic of Victorian schools and had their own purpose. As the wind blasted through the school, wrote Clem Cotterill, one of the first masters, it 'serves but to brace and harden them; to clear their brains and sweeten their tempers; to purify not only their blood, but surely to help, in so far as we can be helped by such agencies, to purify also their hearts.'[2]

The first pupils – 51 boarders, the eldest aged 14 – arrived in 1870 to find Fettes still under construction. 'Ladders and shavings were common in the corridors, and the smell of paint and varnish blended curiously with our strange weird feeling,' wrote one of the 'patriarchs' as these very first 'new men' were to be called. Certain other features of the school were also far from ready; only one of the boarding-houses where the fee-payers were to live was complete, and the great Fettes institution of responsible and mature prefects (young officers in the making) was postponed for half a term when six of the candidates for this office were caught smoking. It was an inauspicious beginning to a tradition based on the first headmaster's belief that a school 'cannot be governed otherwise than by Prefects.'

The uniform consisted of a drab grey suit and a white shirt with Eton collar issued each Saturday night; although it was supposed to last the week, H. Crichton-Miller recalled that 'its pristine glory had generally departed by the Sunday evening.'

Sir Alfred Hamilton Grant remembered above all the temperature:

The dormitories were ice cold and windows were kept open; in the early morning, 7 in so-called summer and 7.30 in very real winter, a cold bath was de rigeur even though the ice required breaking with a hair-brush. No bite or sup passed the lips before first lesson – and cold and empty we ran into College, often through the foulest weather.

Although this particular piece of imperial grittiness has largely passed into history, there are still parts of Fettes where hot taps are welded shut. Gerald FitzGerald Campbell, who became a war correspondent attached to the French armies in the Great War, described the tough conditions which Fettesians experienced:

The whole life of the place was simple and quite sufficiently Spartan. No Fettes boy of those generations will ever forget the east and west winds that swept the field and the front of College in the Spring Term; the daily cold tub in the little flat-bottomed baths in our cubicles; the grind of the paperchases, big and little; the House runs (a later institution) on days too wet or frosty even for Fettes football; the struggle to get the ball when the whole School engaged in punt-about at the same time before serious play began; the coldness of some of the bitter nights of those Edinburgh winters, only on rare occasions mitigated by dormitory fires; the 'plop' of the gas when Skinner, the head porter, or one of his understudies in the Houses, went on their rounds ringing the warning bell in the dark of the early morning; the frenzied rush on empty stomachs to first lesson, 'rep' books in hand; and the simplicity of the fare in hall, intensified now and then by the effort of going without butter for a week in order to pay for the price of fourteen pats, which was the current rate of exchange in the lower forms for one Sunday tart...

There were, too, sundry illicit joys, which called for a certain amount of daring, as when one filched potatoes from the clamps in the fields and cooked them surreptitiously in the classroom fire of one of the less vigilant masters, praying devoutly that the Head might not happen, as he once did, to pay the form a visit and detect the tell-tale smell of roasting. Or you could climb down the rope of the lift in College in the late evening and up again, bringing your sheaves with you. As Froggy Goldschmidt used to say, tenderly fondling the little black ruler with which he occasionally warmed up our cold fingers, 'I don't want to mention any names, Carruthers;' but didn't three warriors once dare the perilous descent, tuck their trousers into their socks, fill them up with apples, and return again rejoicing with over two hundred between them? The gymnastic part of the feat was, of course, nothing like so risky as the adventurous climbs along the third-storey ledges and on the top of the College...

Despite its apparently grim conditions, the school was both academically successful and, by the standards of the time, remarkably cheap. By the 1880s it had grown to 173 pupils, 108 from Scotland, 63 from England, one Irish and one from Italy (albeit with a Scottish mother from Corstorphine); its days as an international school were still a long way off. It was advertised in the *Scotsman* in 1872 as being in Comely Bank 'near Edinburgh'; the entrance fee was ten guineas, tuition in 'Classics, Mathematics, Modern Languages, Natural Sciences, Singing and Gymnastics' cost £25 and boarding – which everyone was expected to do – cost £60. £85 per annum was relatively cheap, certainly for the reasonably comfortable type of clergyman, doctor or solicitor; it is hardly surprising that so many fathers saw the school as a cheap investment. The village schoolmaster and less well-benificed minister might still find places for their sons through the plentiful scholarships, whose recipients were known as foundationers.

The culture of the school was based squarely on Victorian progressivism. Its masters believed in a chivalrous code of behaviour which included temperance, marital fidelity, educational rigour, social duty and religious observation. Fettes College was built on the model of Rugby School and, therefore, aimed squarely at the middle class; this was controversial, since Sir William's will clearly stipulated that his money should be used for the unlucky, with no mention of any fee-payers. There were many, including MPs, ready to criticize the 'Sardanapalian luxury' of Fettes (a cultural reference, obscure even then, to an Assyrian king who lived as 'an effeminate debauchee, sunk in luxury and sloth' – hardly the life of a Fettesian of any era). However, the traditional Scottish free school was in decline and English public schools were on the way up. One of the trustees said Fettes would 'introduce several new features into the educational system of Scotland, and hold forth to large classes of our youth advantages which they do not at present possess elsewhere.'

At Rugby, Dr. Arnold had reformed both conditions and curriculum to create a modern educational institution aimed at moulding Christian gentlemen, for Christian boys, he famously commented, one could scarcely hope to make. C.L.R. James, the great Trinidadian Marxist writer, summarised the great man's goal as the creation of 'a body of men in the upper classes who would resist the crimes of Toryism and the greed and vulgarity of industrialists on the one hand, and the socialistic claims of the oppressed but uneducated masses on the other.'[3] Arnold's pupils would be self-disciplined, self-reliant, able 'to govern themselves so as to be able to govern men.' According to a recent *Guardian* article:

Above all, he made a whole generation of privileged young men realise that they had a moral duty to work for the good of others. While the elite Etonians continued to swirl around in their own moral filth, the subaltern Rugbeians were being trained for a life that was serious, generous and, when necessary, self-sacrificing. It was that moral energy, diffused through Arnold's proteges in the succeeding generation, that transformed the early Victorian ethos of sharp-elbows into a mid-century culture of sterling public service.[4]

Lord Rosebery, a trustee of the school, invited Gladstone himself to Fettes. Prefect Stewart Ponsonby recalled that the great man identified readily with the austere virtues of the school:

He was impressed by the efforts which were being made towards plain living as the handmaid of high thinking. There were rules limiting the amount of money a boy might bring back at the beginning of term. Mr. Gladstone spoke earnestly of the danger of England becoming too rich, and 'sinking' as he put it, 'from her own weight.' The boys all cheered the visitors as they drove off.

At least some of the boys saw the point too. Campbell reflected in the 1920s that:

The ordinary food certainly built up strong bodies and heavy fifteens, and was part of a general system of discipline calculated to teach us to endure hardness and to avoid the snares of luxury. Whether the system was imposed from above or grew out of our own subconscious initiative, all its canons were observed with scrupulous fidelity.

Part of this code, Henry Hamilton Fyfe wrote, was a corporate approach to law and order. A boy convicted by the prefects of particularly heinous acts of bullying could be publicly 'gym-shoed', with every pupil in his house, from the most senior down to 'the smallest urchin', advancing to deliver a blow to the 'criminal'. In 1900, 'Vagabond' contributed a poem to the magazine describing his woes at the bottom of the school's chain of being:

When first I came upon this scene of woe
I thought that I could play the heavy swell,
And do just what I liked; but now I know
The miseries of school-like all too well;
For I became a fag.

Oh! Why should I be made to toast at night?
Why should I dust a lordly prefect's den?
Why light his fire and put his study right?
Why have I got to be in bed by ten
Although I'm but a fag?

This continued for seven more verses, culminating in the poet's account of how he 'tried to play the wag' and suffered a painful meeting with the prefects. But in this, and in another poem in the same vein a few years later, the assumption is that the writer was asking for trouble by being cheeky, and the rest of his house had a good gloat at his deserved fate. That is not to say that there was no bullying: the brutalities of small boys to one another were as frequent at Fettes as elsewhere, as one alumnus wrote:

We were in truth rather a rough-and-tumble lot... small boys of a timid disposition, at all events till they had been at Fettes for more than a term or two, were apt to find life more a vale of tears than a bed of roses. Still, after all, they didn't have such a bad time, and long before they had worked their way up to the top forms and into the leading elevens and fifteens, they were as happy as kings.

A letter home from a small boy of the period survives in the school archives. James Gibson, writing to his mother on 19 December 1898, breathlessly described a crowded life:

It was the quire half and ostercha half Friday, and the ostera had a very nice tea then we practiced two pieces of music which we had to play on Saturday night between the acts of the theatrats it was very good one was "My Uncle Will" the other I forget. I have got a book called "The People of the mist" by H. Rider Haggart. In the exams I am getting on all right except in Euclid which none rarely was able to do and English which a lot of what it was what we had never done, one was an essay on your favourite pastime and I put bycicling (is that rightly spelt) and knowing that Fink liked fishing said that I liked bycicling better than fishing which I thought made you lazy.
I think I have written a long enoght letter today so I will say goodbye I am your loving son
J Gibson
P.S. Only three days more

There is a wistful quality to his final remark – the Christmas holidays were within sight – but the overall tone is recognizable to a parent or teacher of today. The Molesworth spelling may be one reason why the letter was not sent, though it is always possible that a master sensitive to the school's image might have objected to the perennial schoolboy complaint that the exam content had not been covered. Gibson (later a farmer in Tasmania and a sergeant in the Australian Imperial Forces in the First World War) illustrated his letter with a charming picture in the style of Beatrix Potter.

MASTER BAIT   MISS BAIT

James Gibson's drawing in his letter home

For all the faults which Hamilton Fyfe identified in the school (as a left-wing journalist, he found quite a few) he recognized its virtues as well. Much of the moral and physical cruelty associated with boarding schools and brought to public attention during the First World War by Alec Waugh's *The Loom of Youth* was not a feature of Fettes. As J.A. Mangan puts it in his study of public schools and imperialism, Victorian schoolmasters saw themselves as 'the repositories of effective moral education.'[5] Fettes' first headmaster, Dr. Potts, 'a man of high principle, of enlarged and progressive views' had been the sixth form master at Rugby, and was a passionate devotee of the Arnoldian vision. The manly sense of duty which characterised the Fettesian was summed up by Dr. Potts' dying words, read out to the pupils by Alfred Hamilton Grant in the school chapel an hour after his death in 1889:

I wish to offer to all the boys at Fettes College, particularly to those who have been there any time, my grateful acknowledgement of their loyalty, affection and generous appreciation of me. I wish, as a dying man, to record that loving-kindness and mercy have followed me all the days of my life; that faith in God is the sole firm stay in mortal life; that all other ideas than Christ are illusory; and that duty is the one and sole thing worth living for.

Grant, the Head of School (a title changed to Head Boy after the school admitted girls in the 1970s), went on to become a prominent member of the Indian Civil Service, Chief Commissioner of the North-West Frontier and negotiator of the 1919 Treaty with Afghanistan.

Dr Alexander Potts

The pupils were well aware that for Potts, the ideal of duty was not mere rhetoric or humbug. In 1895, one of the patriarchs wrote to the school from India and described his feelings about the death of the Headmaster:

As I glance up from this page, I catch my old Headmaster's eye, looking at me from a very speaking likeness which I am fortunate enough to possess and which stands always on my writing table. I find a solace in that constant companionship.

Sir John Simon, in a letter in 1941, wrote that whenever he visited his old school:

I seem to see the figure of our first headmaster – his flashing eye and the sweep of his gown as he strode up and down, listening to a translation, or his scholarly script as he sat beside you at the centre desk correcting your verses. There can never have been a more inspiring teacher, and his enthusiasm for beauty and truth were positively infectious.

This kind of hero-worship is uncommon today, but it was as important to the Victorian Fettes pupil as it was to the citizen of Sparta or the Roman Republic. W.G. Lely, one of the many Scottish rugby internationals taught at Fettes before the Great War, wrote that David Tanqueray, housemaster of Moredun, 'had the art of inspiring deep affection as well as respect in boys who passed through his hands.' His contemporary K.P. Wilson was remembered with equal respect. The Canadian journalist John Stevenson, recalled that 'there was a fine forthright frankness about him that appealed to boys... Many a Fettesian has had his literature and politics kindled at one of K.P.'s post-Chapel symposia.' These men were, of course, father-figures, all the more so because of the high proportion of pupils who (according to the terms of the foundation) had lost a parent, or, if they were from overseas, might be away from home for years at a time. One Fettes housemaster, responding to a 'pushy' mother who boasted that she had brought up three boys, snorted 'Madam, I've brought up hundreds.'

The boys of Moredun House with their housemaster, David Tanqueray, in 1895; the tiny lad on the far right of the front row is Bertie Anderson, who won the VC in 1918. Second from left at the front is John Erskine Young, the first Fettesian to be killed in the First World War.

In the decade before the outbreak of the First World War, several popular members of staff died suddenly, and the sorrow is clear from the records. In March 1900, George Harrison, housemaster of Glencorse, went down with influenza but, 'anxious as ever not to miss any portion of his work', returned after only two days off and made himself fatally ill. His house, and the 'modern side' pupils to whom he taught geography and history, lost a teacher 'whose friendship was not only kindly but ennobling.' Richard Broadrick was killed, with three other mountaineers, in September 1903 whilst attempting to scale Scafell Pinnacle (a previous Fettes master, F.W. Hill, had narrowly escaped death in the Swiss Alps in an accident which claimed the life of the famous Owen Glynn Jones a few years earlier). Broadrick had been, his obituary recorded, 'the type that boys admire': many-sided, with a love of literature, music, and languages, as well as 'a passion for fresh air and every violent exercise, an ardent enthusiasm for every healthy sport'. One of the other masters wrote:

We have lost a colleague and a master, of whom we had reason to be proud, and our consolation must be that the memory of a noble nature does not end with death, but lives on in finer ideals and loftier aspirations. Terrible and sadly premature as was his death, it was one such as he might well have chosen, in harmony with his character, gallant and fearless as the man himself.

The *Fettesian* carried several poems in his honour, one of which concluded:

Yet his bright courage, steadfast to the end,
Love of the lovely, hatred of the ill,
Shall cheer us through life's struggle, and our friend,
Is with us still.

The most keenly felt loss was probably that of the popular housemaster of Carrington, John Shapland Yeo, in 1904. He had been with the school over twenty years and the boys were 'not merely pupils to him but also his children.' His *Scotsman* obituary described Yeo as 'universally beloved', whilst of his pupils recalled that 'the severest punishment we received was the knowledge that we had hurt him.' He too inspired memorial verse; part of one poem reads:

We, who are old ones now with less to hope
And much more to regret than you can have,
Do charge you now most solemnly to keep
Clear and defin'd his memory in your hearts,
Just as the Greeks of old did carve in stone,
That make men marvel in these latter days,
Statues to heroes whom they lov'd, so you
Carve in your hearts a memory of this man.

Several thousand pounds, raised for a memorial fund by former pupils, was spent on a pavilion and a stained-glass window. In an era when authority is challenged or regarded with cynicism, it is hard for many people to understand the unquestioning loyalty which the officer class of the First World War felt for those above them. It was a concept inculcated at school and constantly reinforced by a culture in wider society which loved heroes and celebrated, for instance, General Gordon and W.G. Grace.

This was not confined to the teaching staff. Successful sportsmen of the sixth form such as Charles Fleming, Vernon Hesketh-Prichard and David Bedell-Sivright were admired to the point of idolatry by the lads. When Fleming died in 1948, a contemporary wrote from Canada that 'the finest flowers of the Fettesian garden are the scholar athletes' and hymned the 'magnificent physique' of this native of Kintyre who captained the Oxford XV (the first Old Fettesian to do so), played for Scotland and then devoted his life to education. Stevenson wrote that whilst 'brains always commanded a certain respect at Fettes' nonetheless 'athletic prowess was the real passport to fame.' His hero-worship of the boys who occupied senior positions when he arrived at the school in 1896 was striking:

The Head of the School was John Lumsden, later a housemaster at Uppingham, who combined great athletic prowess with ample brains. Side was foreign to his nature, and for us youngsters in College he had always a kindly word and a helping hand. But he was merely a demi-god by comparison with the great hero of the School, John Campbell... Endowed with a magnificent physique, he had been in both the cricket and football teams for aeons, and ended his career as Captain of both with the dual School Championship to his credit. He was a born leader of men and boys, and his word was literally law throughout the School, but withal he was a singularly modest boy upon whom his laurels sat lightly, and he well deserved the aura of fame which clung to his name years after his departure.

In 1895, one of the Patriarchs wrote from his Indian bungalow about the latest issue of the *Fettes Register* which enabled him to find out what his contemporaries of 5 October 1870 had got up to. He was notably impressed to see how many of his surviving contemporaries had become ministers of religion: 'so "Kiff" is an archdeacon! ... And "Albe" is a missionary, for the like of which career we marked him out at a very early stage.' The most prominent clergyman, Stewart 'Pon' Ponsonby, he remembered as a wonderful influence on the early school, 'always, and in all things, exercised to forward whatsoever things are noble, and true, and pure, and of good report, and to repress their opposites.'

It is hardly surprising that when, between the wars, Carrington housemaster Harry Pyatt put together a book of Fettes reminiscences, he found that so many OFs had quoted Genesis VI.5 ('There were giants in the earth in those days') that he inserted an index entry: 'Giants, prevalence of.'

An article in the *Fettesian* a few years before the First World War analysed the careers of the 1,613 pupils who had passed through the school's doors since they opened. Of these, 195, well over a tenth, had since died – an indication of Victorian mortality rates, even as they affected the middle and upper classes; the oldest surviving OF at this time was in his fifties – and 54 could not be traced.

The average boy entered Fettes at about thirteen or fourteen and spent four years there, though one managed ten years, leaving when he was 21. About a third of the boys went to university – 184 to Cambridge, 143 to Edinburgh, 132 to Oxford, 76 to other 'Scotch universities' (mostly Glasgow) and 35 to other universities, half of which were in England or Ireland. Almost half of those going to Oxford, and a third of those going to Cambridge, were on scholarships, though former pupils going anywhere else seem to have relied on their own resources. In terms of careers, the single largest group (267, or 15.804 per cent) went into business, followed by the regular 'profession of arms' (180, or 11.184 per cent, of whom about a third were in India), land (144, or 8.923 per cent), law (132, or 8.175 per cent) and engineering (102, or 6.321 per cent).

There were also 92 doctors, 84 bankers and accountants, 55 clergymen (two-thirds of them in the Church of England, a reflection of Fettes' refusal to be pigeonholed as a purely Scottish school), 49 civil servants, 48 teachers (mostly in schools rather than universities) and 40 assorted writers, artists and musicians. Within these groups, 95 were farmers or planters abroad (apart from a few in Argentina, always on 'British soil'), 41 worked as Indian or colonial civil servants, 20 were Indian or colonial police, and ten were engineers for the Public Works Department in the Empire. Outside the armed services, 166 – around an eighth - were involved with the Empire, a slight majority for profit, but at least 71 in some form of public service. The Patriarch of 1895 wrote delightedly:

> ...*it is strange to see how widely scattered over the earth we have become. Assam, Ceylon, Burma, India, Spain, Australia, Gibraltar, Haiti, Java, Canada, Mashonaland, Basutoland – what a list it is! We may well say, 'Quae regio in terris nostri non plena laboris?'* [What region of the earth is not full of our calamities?] *Soldiers and civilians, priests and physicians, lawyers and bankers, engineers and farmers, in how many capacities are we earning our bread and trying, let us hope, to do an honest day's work in the world!*

An example of the Fettesian sense of duty and fair play can be seen in an anecdote about Lewis Robertson, an old boy devoted to sport who joined the army in 1901. It had been a great ambition of his to captain a winning army side against the Royal Navy, and when he was elected captain of army rugby in 1913 it looked as if his dream was going to come true. However, when the great day came to play against the navy before the King in March 1914, another man became available who Robertson considered a better player. 'He was quite prepared,' remembered a contemporary, 'in what he thought were the best interests of the team, to stand down altogether and give up what he had looked forward to for years.'[6]

That the school had done its work was reflected in the memories of former pupils, recorded for posterity in the 1920s. Brigadier-General Robert Carruthers, who served on the North-West Frontier and at Gallipoli, wrote:

> *It was a good school with a fine tone, not, as my readers will perhaps have gathered, from an excess of innate virtue on our part, but because Fettes was leavened by a fine example from the top and because of the strenuous life we were forced to live. Hard work and high morals go hand in hand; and if long school hours, compulsory games, compulsory runs, and*

compulsory paperchases were exacting, and often dull, they left little opportunity for Satan to exploit idle hands.

John Anderson went further:

There may be schools which yield a broader culture and a more generous cultivation of the finer arts, but Fettes provided, in my time, opportunities for an education which was an admirable equipment for the real battle of life. It turned most of its sons loose upon the world with a good physique, a sane and healthy outlook, and a partiality for high emprise in some direction or other; physical weaklings were few, and the prig was indeed a rara avis. But above all, it bred in them a sense of true public spirit and endowed them with a set of traditions of honour and sportsmanship which cling until the grave closes over them...

In a sense Fettes is, to my mind, a microcosm of Scotland in its contribution to the world; it has not produced any supreme artist or original thinker, but it has put forth each year a brood of sons endowed with generous tempers and the gentleman's ideals and standards, who have been equipped to manifest practical competence in some honourable avocation, and usually take with them the foundations of some genuine intellectual interest.

The first pupils and masters at Fettes

2. The Holy Trinity

Like almost all British schoolboys of their time, Fettes pupils had three major influences: the classics, Christianity, and sport. The importance of each of the three varied according to the type of school (some were avowedly secular) and the individual boy, but the ideal might be the first Head of School. William John Lee was 'of good stock', the son and grandson of academically-minded Church of Scotland ministers. Lee won a scholarship to Cambridge and went into the law, devoting himself in retirement to preaching and, during the First World War, the Red Cross, in which capacity he was awarded the OBE. A 'quiet, courteous, scholarly boy', Lee played for the rugby team and in his prefectorial role displayed 'judgment and impartiality.' When Lee left Fettes, Headmaster Dr. Potts told him 'Your career here has been most honourable' – the highest compliment he could give.

Of Lee's varying attributes of classical learning, religious piety, and sporting endeavor, it was the latter which meant most to his fellow-pupils. The outlook of the average British officer in the half-century leading up to the First World War was partly, and often largely, moulded by his experience on the playing fields of his old school. Niall Ferguson has written that 'what made public school products capable of heroism on the Empire's behalf was not what they learned in the classroom, but what they learned on the games field'[7] and this was true for many Fettes boys.

The *Fettesian*, devoted the majority of its pages to detailed accounts of team games, with the First XIs and XVs given honoured place as the school's heroes. These reports reflect a world in which key values of team spirit, tactical thought, and physical fitness were taught on the hallowed turf. C.L.R. James, who devoted much of his adult life to ending the British Empire, was given a comprehensive training in its athletic underpinnings at his public school in Trinidad, and wrote one of the greatest books on cricket ever penned. Despite, or because of, his Marxist political leanings, he saw cricket in particular as imparting the Puritan values of restraint, honesty, teamwork, patience and skill born of incessant practice, and thus as one of the pillars of what the Empire's supporters saw as its moral justification.[8] The recollections of Fettes pupils of this era suggest that cricket was popular, but that Fettes was not so successful in this field as in rugby: 'in most seasons the defeats appear to outnumber the victories' wrote Sir George Gillen, a cricketing pupil in the 1900s, who blamed the Scottish climate. The school did, however, produce a few notable cricketers such as Malcolm Jardine and Vernon Hesketh Prichard.

The Victorians and Edwardians loved sport and spent a great deal of time codifying it, setting up the leagues and competitions which exist to this day, and celebrating it in their popular culture. Hely Hutchinson Almond, Headmaster of Fettes' neighbour Loretto, saw 'the training of the governing class' primarily in terms of strength of will and body rather than cleverness. 'I would rather have a school of dull boys than of clever ones,' he once wrote to a parent.[9] Physical fitness would be welded to *espirit de corps* and self-sacrifice so that his Christian soldiers would go throughout the Empire 'spreading the contagion of their vigour.'[10] In flagrant opposition to the thinking of the Army reformers, Almond wanted *less* academic study for Sandhurst rather than more – football and hunting would be far better training for young officers, imparting as they did teamwork, instinct, healthiness and endurance.

At Fettes, he was warmly admired by many. When he died, the *Fettesian* editor described him as 'one who stood out as champion of all that was noblest in public school life' and that the sermons he preached on his visits to Comely Bank would 'never be recalled save with feelings of deep veneration.' His keenest disciple was Clem Cotterill, Housemaster of Glencorse, author of *Suggested Reforms in Public Schools*, where he described the wonders wrought by the hour's daily exercise he imposed on his boys. Cotterill was all for character:

Cleverness – what an aim! Good God, what an aim! Cleverness neither makes nor keeps man or nation. Let it not be thought that it ever can. For a while it may succeed, but only for a while. But self-sacrifice – this it is that makes and preserves men and nations, yes, and fills them with joy – only this. Big brains, and big biceps – yes, both are well enough. But courage and kindness, gentle manliness, and self-sacrifice – this is what we want.[11]

Cotterill's gentle manliness went to the extent of taking his coat off and getting involved in a punch-up when an argument with a referee during a match between Fettes and another school 'turned sanguinary'. He once famously told his pupils that 'there will be a voluntary run tomorrow afternoon for this house, and if any boy does not go I will flog him within an inch of his life.'

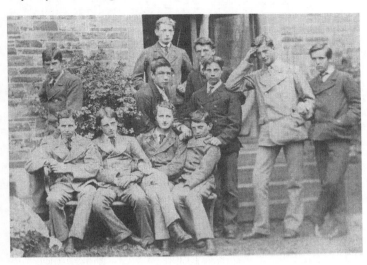

Clem Cotterill (seated, third from left) and pupils; standing second from right is Stewart Ponsonby, captain of football and cricket, prefect, vicar, and hero to a generation of younger boys.

There was no place for mere spectators in this world of sport – Lord Baden-Powell specifically identified watching, as opposed to participating in, games (along with loafing, smoking, socialism and masturbation) as one of the prime sources of British decadence which his Scouting movement was intended to curtail. Moreover, games were preferred which encouraged either physical toughness or teamwork (ideally both) and which brought glory upon one's house. Henry Hamilton Fyfe recalled that tennis was frowned upon as it did no one any good but those playing it; games were a 'corporate duty' owed to one's house, 'our little State within a State.'

A more acceptable form of individual exercise was the whole-school run. Gerald FitzGerald Campbell described this with some relish: 'In the Christmas term the hardening process began, almost directly we came back from the summer holidays, with four or five paperchases of surprising length.' These took boys out to the shores of the Forth, to Davidson's Mains, Corstorphine Tower, Cramond Bridge and other beauty spots some distance from the school. Younger boys believed that the distance covered was around eighteen or twenty miles, but the official report for the 1902 run says it was more like sixteen. Not only were they plodding across miles of ploughed fields, they often had to ford 'the rushing torrent' of the Water of Leith or River Almond, or swim across the Union Canal, pausing only for 'the ravenous gnawing by chattering teeth of turnips, apples, and other windfalls, or better still, the sticky consumption of a 'jeely-piece' at the grocer's shop in some outlying village'. If lucky, there was a hot bath when they staggered home, and the top six had the pride of reading their names pinned to the notice-board outside the dining-hall before tea. 'What fun it all was, and what good sport,' wrote Campbell, 'and what a test and training in endurance and grit and agility and the quick use of your intelligence.'

It was rugby, above all, which the school celebrated, and following enthusiastically after their neighbours, Edinburgh Academy, Fettesians helped develop the game in Scotland. Before the First World War, no less than 37 played for Scotland, and three for England, including household names like Andrew 'Bunny' Don-Wauchope and David 'Darkie' Bedell-Sivright. By the outbreak of the Second World War the school had produced over fifty internationals, mostly for Scotland but also one Irish and four English. It was a source of shame for Fettesians of a particular era if their generation did not produce stars. A former pupil who attended the school in the mid-1890s was embarrassed to record that:

> In 1891, both the Oxford cricket and rugby teams were captained by Fettesians, (Malcolm Jardine and Charles Fleming). However, in the 1890s games declined, with no Fettesian Blue at Cambridge between 1893 and 1897, or Oxford from 1892 to 1899; nor did any new Scottish internationals appear from Fettes. The situation was remedied when Fleming returned to the school as a master and made games teaching more rigorous and professional.

In 1905, New Zealand played a Scotland side with six Old Fettesians, and the following year five represented their country against South Africa; in the last Calcutta Cup before war broke out two former pupils were on the field. Despite the enthusiasm of popular housemaster K.P. Wilson for the game, association football never really caught on, but teams did appear, one of which took on the mighty Hearts, who duly thrashed them 8-2 in 1878.

The *Fettesian* regularly carried poems about sport, which vied with the classics, affectionate gripes about school life, and imperialism for the position of favourite theme for young bards. Rugby, of course, and school spirit were popular:

Same old goals on the same old ground,
Same old backers with the same old sound,
Same old yelling when the halves run round!
Same old Fettes,
Ready to do or die!
Same old Fettes,
As it was in the days gone by!
Every time the flags are set
Down the touch-lines, don't forget
It's the same old Fettes!

Contemporary sporting news often received attention, such as a 1904 ode to the amateur golf champion, subtitled 'A Travisty' after the American player who enjoyed considerable success with the controversial new Schenectady putter. Cricket was the subject of this rather charming poem which appeared at the same time:

Sunshine bright or meagre,
Good or bad the day,
Weather-careless, eager,
Youth goes out to play.
Clouds may lift or lower,
Still the cry's the same,
'What's the wicket matter?
Come and play the game.'

'How's that?' – 'Over' – thud of bat on leather,
Driving haar above you or a hot June sun;
Ring of merry voices that the breezes blend together –
Let the echoes linger when the game is done.

Bowlers all beset you,
Bowlers slow or fast;
One is bound to get you
Out somehow at last.
Luck may stay or shun you,
Nobody's to blame:

Win or lose – what matter?
If you play the game.

Wind and trees and greensward – cheers and sunny laughter,
Clapping in the distance where the scores mount high –
Will you quite forget them in the days that follow after?
Will the vision linger as the years glide by?

Golden youth unheeded,
Lessons you may see,
Comfort you when needed
Through the years to be.
Heart and hand be steady,
Straight and sure your aim;
Rise or fall – what matter?
Only play the game.

'How's that?' – 'Over' – thud of bat on letter,
Wickets clicking round you as the games go on;
Ring of merry voices that the breezes blend together –
Let the echoes linger when your youth is gone.

Published ten years before the outbreak of the Great War, this poem has unmistakable echoes of Newbolt's schoolboy call to play up and play the game, published in 1892. 'Vitaï Lampada' has been much mocked by posterity, but sporting metaphors and ideals were common in the letters of former Fettesians who wrote to the school about their adventures. George Dillon of the 26th Punjab Infantry was desperately keen to lead his men against a 'refractory tribe of wild hillmen, who thought fit to molest us', but on tenterhooks in case he was told to stay behind and look after the post: 'my feelings were something like the day when Pon [Stewart Ponsonby] told me I should have my cap if I played well.' A letter from Donald Watt in Jambatai Kotai in 1895 describes being hit by a bullet which had already passed through a comrade's brain as 'just like a tremendous "hack" at football. It made me feel a bit queer.'

School loyalty was also inculcated through sport. The explorer Vernon Hesketh-Prichard, whilst a pupil at Fettes, turned down the chance to play for Scotland against South Africa, on the grounds that his school need him for a match against Loretto, and that was where his loyalty must lie. In both world wars, former pupils serving overseas avidly read the school magazine to see how their houses had performed in the annual 'belows' competitions, and how Fettes had performed against the Academy, Loretto, Watson's, and Merchiston. Sir John Simon, although not an especially gifted footballer or cricketer, displayed to the end of his life a certain irritation if Monday's *Times* did not carry reports of Fettesian sporting engagements.

The quintessential Britishness of such attitudes contributed to a sense of national distinctiveness. W.K. McClure, an Old Fettesian reporting on the war in North Africa in 1912, appreciated that his readers might find it strange that Italian troops, in moments of boredom, built elaborate sandcastles: 'British soldiers, in similar circumstances, would have organised cricket or football matches; but the Italian is not a player of outdoor games.'[12] A great admirer of the Italians, he insisted that this in no way meant they were inferior fighting men who were letting the European side down, suggesting that whilst the Arabs may indeed have thought the soldiers' activities odd, 'some of our most popular amusements may have excited similar feelings in Oriental minds.'

Robert Bruce Lockhart, in pre-war Moscow, was invited to play for a local team, the Morozovtsi, set up by a British industrialist 'as an antidote to vodka drinking and political agitation'.[13] Lockhart had, in fact, been mixed up with his brother, a gifted sportsman at Cambridge, and was in any case more of a rugger than soccer man, but, like all Fettesians, 'always ripe for adventure', he accepted. In any case, 'five years in the worship of athleticism' at Fettes had prepared him for anything. Football mythology has it that when the Charnocks initially punted a ball in the direction of the Russian spectators they fled, believing it was one of the spherical bombs favoured by anarchists.

Lockhart's experiences led him to a conclusion not dissimilar to that of the British politicians who considered sending a cricket team to revolutionary France: 'If it had been adopted in other mills, the effect on the character of the Russian working-men might have been far-reaching.'[14] Although this may be debatable, there is no doubt that sport played a valuable role in imperial unity, transcending racial divisions, especially in cricket; as Ferguson puts it, 'the English habit of losing to colonial teams would help knit Greater Britain together.'[15]

For the less athletic, however, this obsession could make schooldays a nightmare; one asportual OF calling himself 'Litterae Inhumaniores' wrote in 1906 that:

A Balliol scholarship will hardly compensate for an entire indifference to games. It is exhausting to have to go through school life like one on a secret errand. How often as I passed the haven of the sixth-form library did I taste the bitterness of Balzac's cry, 'Sans genie, je suis flambé!' I hope I wasn't a prig, I know that I was unhappy.

Henry Hamilton Fyfe also had his doubts, writing that 'I cannot deny that most of us Fettesians of that period were deplorably underdeveloped on our intellectual and emotional sides' and noting with regret of the 'meagre list of the early Fettes boys who made themselves prominent in Literature, Art, Politics, or the Law' in contrast with the huge number of soldiers whose adventures were trumpeted in the school magazine.

However, the school's culture was not as anti-intellectual as these rare criticisms suggest. The boys and masters of Fettes College believed that their rugby and cricket, their athletics and their football, and all the obsessions which went with these sports, were rooted in the classics, which were the core of the curriculum. C.L.R. James linked Britain's national celebration of W.G. Grace's hundredth century in 1895 with the ancient Greek city-states, which saw a national victory by one of their athletes as 'a testament to the quality of the citizens.'[16] Robert Bruce Lockhart recalled that at Fettes, 'for all the school's reputation for 'rugger', brawn, except in a few rare instances, was never cultivated at the expense of brain, and I know no school to which Kipling's stricture of 'muddied oafs' applied less.'[17] Glencorse housemaster K.P. Wilson made it clear that 'nothing repelled him so much as the athletic "blood" who regarded games as the end-all of existence and despised books.' As Stevenson recalled:

[Scholarship] *boys in College probably worked harder than elsewhere, because most of them had to face the world with few financial resources, and more depended upon the use they made of their time at School. But nowhere in the school was laziness accounted a virtue, and the intellectual pabulum was delicately graded to suit a variety of appetites.*

Arnold himself had been solely concerned with spiritual and intellectual development, and seems to have had an almost Platonic notion that the function of schooling was to train a bunch of Godly philosopher-kings rather than muddied oafs or flannelled fools. His successors, Potts included, preferred the development of all-round character – flannelled philosophers, perhaps. John Yeo, one of Fettes' most popular housemasters, was undoubtedly a man in this mould. Whilst he 'really liked fielding cover-point on a raw day or going for a run in a blizzard' he was also 'a genius at expounding mathematical problems.'[18] When he died in 1904, a substantial cricket pavilion was erected in his honour from funds raised by admiring former pupils. Although Dr. Potts was a good friend of the sports-fanatic Cotterill, and himself a promoter of vigorous exercise, he did not share the housemaster's distrust of brains. When Potts died, the governors did consider Cotterill – who saw himself as the natural successor – but then considered his opinions on abolishing competitive examinations and his poor discipline in lessons, and opted for the more academic Rev. Dr. Heard.

Central to intellectual endeavour were the classics, and these were taught by the headmaster in the Upper, a large classroom with a surprisingly modern horseshoe-shaped desk rather than the traditional rows. 'Reading the *Republic* or Cicero's *De Natura Deorum* with the Head was like having windows opened on to eternal oceans of speculation, eternal mountain ranges of earnest thought,' as even the critical Hamilton Fyfe admitted.[19] The classics were the path to true intellectual enlightenment and civilisation, as H.W. Auden, a former Fettes master, wrote in 1906:

The genius of the people, with its instinct for beauty, its versatility, its keen sense of proportion, raised them to such a high degree of civilization, that in art, philosophy, literature, and all the higher spheres of thought, their influence on the world has surpassed that of any other nation. Greek literature is the fountain-head of all western literature... we are intellectually the direct descendants of the ancient Greeks. Greek civilization has made us what we are in thought and feeling.[20]

A former pupil wrote that Potts' successor, William Heard, who saw the school through the Great War and died shortly afterwards, 'set less store on the Classics as an exercise in elegant scholarship than as an eternal fountain of light and guidance for the problems of the modern world.' Robert Philp, who taught at Fettes from the 1960s and later wrote the school's official history, explains the rationale behind the classical obsession:

When the great Classical Headmasters of Fettes laid down their Classical regimen, they believed that they were not only making their charges more scholarly, more thorough and accurate, but that they were actually making them better citizens... To them the Classical training was something of a gospel, taught in the conviction that the future character of their charges depended on their teaching. Even the business of grammar and syntax maybe had its bearing on later life. As he battled through the jungle of gerunds or the mass of Oratio Obliqua, *the Fettesian might be showing the very fibre that would fit him to administer a colony or sit on the Bench. The training was general, befitting the future of a wide and varied empire.*[21]

Sir John Simon remembered with admiration 'The Book' in which boys were invited by the headmaster to write Latin and Greek compositions. 'One read with awe the recorded efforts of giants,' he wrote. He was, admittedly, a very academic scholarship boy who may not have been wholly representative, but contemporary readers of this hallowed relic are invariably impressed. By contrast, Cecil Reddie, an early pupil of Fettes who returned as a progressive master in 1885, saw classicism as merely the undesirable twin of team games:

The type of mind which excels at the 'classics' is by no means of necessity the highest; in some cases it is the least original, least vigorous, least complex. Hence the docility of the pupil... There is considerable analogy between the cram of athletics and the cram of 'classics.' The boys are tied down, with little regard to individual tastes, to playing the same few games. And these — mainly Cricket and Football — are highly elaborate and artificial... They should have a wider horizon than the walls of the playing-fields.[22]

It is undoubtedly true that there was something of a caste system in the sixth form at Fettes; those who took modern languages and science ('Mods') rather than Latin and Greek (the 'Classical Sixth') were subject to petty acts of discrimination such as being denied hot milk. Dr. Heard referred to them as 'barbarians', and it was widely believed that the resignation of the popular German teacher Vivian Phillipps – who went on to become a lawyer and Liberal chief whip – was because he had been bypassed for promotion by a less experienced classicist. Alan Campbell Swinton, who, whilst a schoolboy in 1879, read a description of the telephone (invented in 1877) and promptly built one to link Glencorse and Moredun Houses – the first telephone in Scotland. He was equally promptly told to dismantle it and get back to his Latin.[23]

None of this seems to have prevented Fettes from producing a steady stream of doctors, engineers, artillerymen and scientists. Boys were free to pursue their technical interests at home, and James Gibson was clear in his 1898 letter how he planned to spend Christmas:

> I want you to make up all the money I owe you so that I may pay it all at once, I will have eight or nine shillings when I come home and I am going to get a stationary engine I think which is 7/6 post 6d and a circular saw for it to work 1/11 so I think I will have to break into that five shilling bit you have got I think this is a good engine I am going to get, it is 13½ inches height and the fly-wheel is 3½ inches in dimater I am going to try and get the catalog.

Swinton later distinguished himself as a pioneer of x-rays and television. Reddie departed to set up his own school at Abbotsholme, which – although aimed at training a new elite through modern methods – never saw its alumni scale the heights of military and imperial glory which Fettesians conquered. But then, as Hamilton Fyfe admitted, 'He was not, for some reason, popular – perhaps, at first, because he objected to our time in the Laboratory being occupied in the production of horrible smells. More probably his ideas were found repellent.'

Reddie also disapproved of institutional religion, and flirted with a kind of pantheism; Abbotsholme's symbol was the Star of Solomon, religious education featured a wide variety of faiths, and he was buried on a hill in the grounds beneath a distinctly pagan stone slab. Dr. Potts, by contrast, was a man of very traditional, though non-sectarian, Christian outlook. His personal holiness was such that Noel Paton is believed to have hoped to use him as a model in a painting of Christ. Had he not died early, Potts would have gone from Fettes to the ministry of the Church of England, where he would teach the Bible story to poor children in parish schools. His successor, William Heard, was a clergyman, and he in turn was replaced by Alec Ashcroft, whose ideas resembled Christian socialism.

Until after the Second World War, the headmaster of Fettes was his own chaplain, taking brief services each morning in a chapel which was literally the spine of the main building. On Sundays, the boys went to Church of Scotland or Episcopalian services in Edinburgh according to family traditions. The trial of having to walk through the streets of Edinburgh in top hat and tails was rewarded by the entertaining, inspirational sermons of the Rev. Lauchlan Maclean Watt at St. Stephen's, and indeed the presence of young women in the congregation. To this day some of their graffiti adorns what were then the upstairs pews in the church. This was followed by an evening service in the school chapel, 'one of the workshops in which the life of Fettes was fashioned'. Despite the devout Anglicanism of the first three heads, this was non-denominational. It was here that the headmaster's sermons were delivered, the favourite theme of Heard's being 'that a standard of Christian conduct was essential for a happy life.' On one occasion the headmaster was upstaged, when on 22 May 1887 Mr. Huxtable, the music master, collapsed and died whilst playing the organ.

The memories of former pupils and the number who went into ordained ministry suggests that, although bringing up religion in conversation was seen as rather bad form, Fettes did not merely pay lip-service to Christianity. Grant recalled that 'the moral tone at Fettes was excellent' and Hamilton Fyfe remembered the masters made clear that 'there was a choice between behaving decently and behaving like cads.' Of Heard, he wrote that 'his sermons at Sunday evening Chapel planted in many immature minds the seeds of that religion shared, despite differences of belief and observance, by all who seek some aim in life beyond self-indulgence... He lifted us into a region where dogma counted for little, duty for much.'

One of the many who went from Fettes to Christian ministry was Charles Bowden; head of school and winner of prizes for Latin hexameters, he emigrated to New Zealand a few years after leaving university, and was ordained as an Anglican clergyman. Known for 'a genuine kindness and thoughtfulness, especially towards the sick and suffering', he believed, like his old headmaster Dr. Potts, that 'the only true standard of life is the standard of the Gospel'. Bowden died after continuing to work despite having taken ill, and died in 1909: 'he practically gave his life for the cause,' as Archdeacon Averill put it at his funeral.[24] Bowden was in his forties when he died. His near-contemporary, Gilbert White, became the first Bishop of Carpentaria, and his approach to the Aboriginal population there reflected Fettesian values of social duty driven by undogmatic Christianity. Noting that the Aborigines were the 'original owners and inhabitants' of Australia, dispossessed by the white man and living in poverty, White argued for prioritising their needs:

There is an element of justice, of reparation, of plain and obvious duty to this work which commends itself to the most hardened man of the world who cannot enter into the enthusiasm of the Gospel... What we want is to develop the Aborigines and half-castes in such a way that they may be fitted to hold their own in future, and to make them of real service to the state, while increasing and developing their self-respect.[25]

The simple faith of many of these pre-war pupils was recalled in the *Fettesian* in 1948, in a rather less religious age. Cyril Lely, writing of his contemporary Bertie Anderson, who won the Victoria Cross in the Spring Offensive at the Somme in 1918, remembered a 'quiet-spoken lad' who at bedtime in the tiny top dormitory in Moredun would simply say 'Dix' – the school code for temporary silence – and proceed to say his prayers. That is not to say that all of the pupils were saintly, or otherwise perfect specimens; one OF, reflecting on news from the school of the death of a contemporary, wrote:

So poor old Chimpanzee was killed by the bursting of a boiler, was he? Well, some of us can remember how often he blew himself up, with less serious results, in his study. I recall him as of gigantic size, and I suppose he really was big for his age. I think of the awe with which a circle of very small boys heard him declare at the end of his last term at school that if his master kept him back for his 'lines', he would knock him down and walk to his home in Edinburgh. I have no doubt he was kept back – he always was – the poor Chimpanzee had no memory; but his exit was quite peaceful and law-abiding. As I write I suddenly recall his mysterious power of wagging his ears, which he delighted to display.

On the whole, though, former pupils were clear about Fettes' generously-defined Christian ethos. Heard, who 'set a noble example of such conduct' had, like Potts, an enduring influence:

It began while they were still at School, and was found in every House, every Form room, and every generation, and the tone which they took with them into the outer world was clean, manly and wholesome. That was true, not only of the scholars and athletes, but, with hardly an exception, of the great bulk of those with whom they worked and played shoulder to shoulder.

The school chapel in the 1880s

3. Fettes and Empire

The British Empire is not one of the most fashionable institutions to defend these days, enthusiastically though some have tried. It often ruthlessly exploited its subject peoples, imposing alien economic and cultural values on them. The slave trade of the eighteenth century and famines of the nineteenth killed millions. It has also been argued that it was not particularly good for the British themselves, leaving, even unto the third generation, an entirely unwarranted sense of superiority over others, a false sense of commercial complacency and an inability to face reality. Even Niall Ferguson refers to the swarming of the British across the globe as a 'white plague'.

Most Fettesians in the decades before the Great War, however, saw nothing wrong with the Empire. The values they imbibed at school prepared them to support and serve it. A group of schoolboy poets ('T, etc.') in the *Fettesian* of March 1899, could, in their verses entitled *Adventurers*, illustrate how idealistic patriotism blended with national acquisitiveness and Social Darwinism in the imperial mission:

For her we wandered, and for her we died,
And to her we brought our trophies red;
For her we bargained, fought and strove and tried,
That unto her our honour might be wed.

By land we lost our lives amid the snows
That lie above the sunny Indian plains;
Backwards we rolled the war-might of our foes,
Or left our bones to rot 'neath Burma's rains.

We brought her merchandise, we brought her gold,
Our chosen strength we sold to work her will.
By war, red war, the lands we won we'll hold
Through storm or fair, through good report or ill.

We are her power, hers hold we in our hand;
So shall it be until the end of all.
With hand on sword we guard our native land,
And gladly die, if once we hear her call.

The fact that this poem was on the first page of the *Fettesian* speaks volumes for the opinions of the time. When the boys wrote about the Empire (which was often) they tended to use allusions which connected it to the civilizing mission of their classical heroes. 'Delhi', an 81-line poem by Archibald Young Campbell (later a distinguished poet, academic, and friend of Rupert Brooke) appeared in the *Fettesian* in 1904, following the Coronation Durbar. Summarising the history of the city, the poem made clear that British rule was best, and that if this needed to be imposed by force, so be it. It won the school prize for poetry and undoubtedly has a certain dark beauty:

'Long live the King' From every bright bazaar,
From each throng'd street with glittering standards hung
The acclaim goes up. They hear it from afar –
Those immemorial ruins that have rung
With like gay clamours in another tongue
Long ages past. Renew'd it swells amain
Temples and mosques and ancient tombs among,
And columns huge, that crumbling long have lain,
Echo 'God save our King and emperor!' again.

So pageantry once more in Delhi shines,
So Jumna's banks keep holiday once more;
And curious eyes are wondering at the shrines
Where the swart Moslem kissed the marble floor,
Or in the courts the Mongol kept before
With lingering gaze the faded splendour scan.
Sounds of assembled races thunder o'er
The slumbering heads of Baber and Jehan:
They triumphed in their day, the kings of Hindustan.

There was a time when still the giant beast
Whose bright-draped flanks oft deck'd the despot's train –
Fit sign of cumbrous rule in that rich East –
Moved in primeval jungle and lone plain
Untroubled; seeking now through deep lane
His peers, a dusky troop in dusky glade
Gambolling mightily; or now was fain
To flee the noon in cool delightful shade,
Or slowly in some pool his monstrous limbs he laid.

Then India shone with labours wrought in peace,
Not glittered with a tyrant conqueror's spoil,

Her only wealth the bountiful increase
That Nature and a glad unravaged soil
Brought forth to cheer the patient Hindu's toil:
Nor knew the desolation that intrudes
On happy homes, nor dreamed of war's turmoil.
Still the rank undergrowth in all the woods
Ran free, and blossom filled their fragrant solitudes.

But southward sounds the clash of Tarta drums,
On Himalayan peaks dark war-clouds loom;
Lo! Timur through the Vale of Roses comes,
And stains it redder than the rose's bloom.
That same Mongolian race, opposing whom
The Great Wall fell, impending like a storm,
Darken the sunny fields with awful gloom
They burst. In Delhi murderous squadrons swarm,
And the Five Rivers flow with crimson flood and warm.

So the lame victor topp'd the cone of skulls –
His work on earth – and hobbled underground;
And after him a host of Grand Moguls.
And now in turn the times of wealth came round,
And now of woe. For mastery of the ground
Magnificence and carnage ever vied.
Where Timur slew, Baber did empire found,
And perish'd. Shah Jehan, too, in his pride
Built him a city, walled and gated, and he died.

The Western came, with Industry and Law;
Fought, seized and Ind for his dominion took;
And ninety years and nine revolving saw
Her troublous land a peaceful ruler brook.
Yet since the intemperate winds heed not rebuke,
Nor iron bonds control the wilful main,
She with one impulse off their lordship shook;
Fierce, restless hearts, impatient of the chain,
Rebelled, and Delhi was her lawless self again.

The Eastern sun that burns men's brows with flame,
And tempers steely cheeks beneath his fire,
Yet deeper smites, enkindling all their frame,
In their impetuous souls his breath to inspire.
They raged. The avenger, cooler and more dire,
Master of vast premeditated stroke,

42

Quelled their hot fury with his paler ire:
Delhi like steed or stubborn ox he broke,
So freed her from herself beneath his gentle yoke.

As barbarous in that last barbaric stand,
So barbarous in thy loyalest display,
City or reign and ruin! This fair land
Itself not such another Durbar day
Shall know. The age of pageants dies away;
Yet may our Western rule new glories rear
And his much wisdom prove who once did say,
Gilding his cornice with the legend clear:
'If there's a paradise on earth, 'tis here, 'tis here!'

Fettes alumni proudly served this imperium in the British Army, the Indian Army, the Indian Civil Service, the British Civil Service, the Volunteers and assorted colonial militias. They were doctors, schoolmasters, administrators, merchants, planters, soldiers and missionaries. Empire meant adventure, and Fettesians undoubtedly caught the fever of excitement when one of their number, Donald Watt of the King's Own Scottish Borderers, was pictured in the *Daily Graphic* fighting off three Pathans in the Malakand Pass single-handed.

For Fettesians and other educated Britons, one of the most important and prestigious forms of imperialism was the work of the Indian Civil Service, a small elite of about a thousand highly-trained professionals who ruled over three hundred million Indians. Clive Dewey summarises the position of the Civilians, as its officials were known:

They collected the revenue, allocated rights in land, relieved famines, improved agriculture, built public works, suppressed revolts, drafted laws, investigated crimes, judged lawsuits, inspected municipalities, schools, hospitals cooperatives – the list is endless. The long lines of petitioners, choking their verandahs and waiting patiently outside their tents, paid tribute to their power.[26]

Whilst it should be borne in mind that the Civilians were not entirely alone in their work – they had a significant number of local clerks to help them, the so-called 'brown sahibs' who would later aspire to rule India themselves – there is still something extraordinary about this tough and high-minded caste. Jan Morris notes that in the prestigious Indian Civil

43

Service examinations 'it was rare to find two entries in one year from the same school'[27] but Fettes provided an extraordinary number, each issue of the magazine reporting on their successes in it; in June 1891, for instance, it reported that W. Grindlay, A. Duff, and W. Morison had come in the top twenty of the Indian Civil Service examinations, and would shortly be posted to Bengal, the Punjab, and Bombay, respectively. Robert Bruce Lockhart recalled that the coach for the Indian Civil Service examination recommended fathers who wanted their sons to pursue this career should send them to Fettes – 'the education there is the best that I know of.'[28]

As Clive Dewey has explained in his study of the ICS, it was an extraordinarily intellectual organization – despite its members' desire to be seen as rugged men of action, the academic ability they possessed was second to none. To get in and get on, successful Civilians needed to amass, analyse and interpret vast quantities of data and create from it concrete proposals; they had to suggest possible solutions to complex problems, weighing up various options; they needed to refine and explain policy.[29] A Fettes education, which emphasized physical and moral rigour, literary and linguistic analysis, capacious memory skills, and dexterity in advancing an argument, was an ideal background for this. In 1908 there were enough OFs in the ICS and Indian Army at Pachmarhi alone (and not only that, but for them to have been contemporaries in Carrington House) for there to be a Fettes polo team; it reached the finals of the local tournament.

Thanks to the school's archives, we have several examples of the work of Fettesian members of the ICS in the decades before the First World War. Patriarch Alan Duff, Deputy Commissioner at Jubbulpore, died aged 36 in 1897 of 'brain fever brought on by overwork' during the terrible famine of that year. He was, 'though half-unconscious, constantly planning relief works, or forming schemes to save his district from want.' His wife died two months later as a result of the disease which ravaged the land in the famine's wake. Although the British handling of the disaster has been severely criticised, this popular and able man genuinely believed he was there to help.

So too did his fellow-patriarch John Campbell Arbuthnot, who in that same year was Deputy Commissioner at Shillong, which was devastated by one of the most dramatic recorded earthquakes in Indian history. 'Mr. Arbuthnot, who, with his wife and children, had a very narrow escape, greatly distinguished himself by the prompt and vigorous measures he took to combat the terrible effects of the earthquake.'[30] His valete in *The Englishman* described events:

Houses and offices came tumbling about the ears of great and small, and if anyone under such circumstances lost his presence of mind it was surely excusable, but not so the D.C. He was out day and night working to rescue the dead and injured from the fallen ruins, and organising shelter and food for the survivors amid the torrents of rain and repeated severe shocks of earthquake which continued after the great catastrophe.

One of the earliest pupils of the school, Arbuthnot went on to become the longest-serving member of the ICS, having learned Persian, Kassia, Garo, and Miri, and gained an encyclopaedic knowledge of the tribes of Assam and the Frontier; he retired just as the Great War broke out. Another Old Fettesian, serving as a diplomat in Italy, was killed in the great Messina earthquake of 1908.

In some overseas territories, the British did not govern directly, but had a Resident who 'advised' the local ruler. One such was Douglas Graham Campbell, who left Schoolhouse at Fettes in 1883 and went straight into the administrative service of the Federated Malay States as a surveyor. He quickly role through the ranks, becoming first the secretary to the Resident of Selangor, then a district officer, and eventually the Resident of Negri Sembilan. In 1906 he played an important role in the negotiations which placed Brunei under British protection whilst preserving the authority of its Sultan. His skills impressed the Governor, who in 1910 appointed him as the first adviser to the Sultan of Johore, a prickly individual who had both irritated the British by flirting with an independent economic policy and neglected his subjects, and indeed the state finances, by going on extensive overseas trips.

Campbell's obituary (he died in harness, of fever in 1918, aged 50) noted that he combined *suaviter in modo* with *fortiter in re* (gentle in manner, strong in deed). In 1912, he fell out with Sultan Ibrahim over malpractices in the local prison; Cambell wanted the British to extend their administrative control of Johore to remedy these and other abuses, whilst the Sultan wanted greater independence. Campbell won, but out of deference to the Sultan's status he retained the title of General Adviser rather than being officially upgraded to Resident. Under Campbell's guidance, Johore became more prosperous, though it

is possible that there was a degree of wishful thinking in the
Straits Times obituary:

> *From his own report penned early last year the State, in
> spite of the War, has enjoyed a period of exceptional and
> increasing prosperity, the value of the exports last year
> increasing by $12,943,980 as compared to the previous year,
> flattering testimony to a regime which has been uniformly
> successful. His Highness the Sultan has lost his right hand man,
> and the State has lost a faithful, upright and loyal servant.*[31]

The Sultan quarrelled so frequently with Campbell's
successors that five were appointed in quick succession, however,
by the 1950s, possibly with the instructive experience of
Japanese occupation behind him, he was lobbying against
Malaysian nationalists to retain the Adviser.

Maintaining order was another important role for the
Fettesian overseas. W.E. Wait, an OF based in Ceylon, wrote to
the school to describe how, in June 1903, he and two local
policemen had to try to deal with a riot against Roman Catholics
by Buddhist agitators; rather than risk deaths, he 'tried a bit of
bluff' by pointing unloaded rifles at the mob sacking the
parsonage, and was relieved to see the troublemakers bolt. He
then cycled round the city ensuring the safety of the nuns and
organising local headmen to keep their people quiet.

Not everyone could hack imperial life. Douglas Gordon
Schulze was one of the many rugby internationals produced by
the school at the turn of the century and, on graduation from
Merton College, Oxford, was destined for a career as a colonial
school inspector. He arrived in Rangoon on 7 June 1908 and
resigned a fortnight later – not even an interview with the
Lieutenant Governor could change his mind, and by early July he
was on the boat home, happy to reimburse the £47 6s. travelling
expenses.[32] He prudently changed his surname to Miller in the
xenophobic days of 1919, by which time he had become Rector of
Kelvinside Academy in Glasgow; he was subsequently
Headmaster of Aberdeen and then Manchester Grammar
Schools. The great Charlie Fleming, another international rugby
player, had returned to Fettes as a master (interestingly,
remembered as the only member of staff in the 1890s with a
strong Scots accent). He went out to Sudan in 1900 but, as an
'incurable northerner' he 'found the tropical heat of the Sudan so
constantly irksome that he resigned.'

James Currie clearly found the climate more bearable; he became principal of Gordon College, Khartoum, and developed Sudanese educational policy up to the First World War. Although his approach seems rather limited by today's standards (Currie had no plans to educate the locals, except for a small 'native administrative class', beyond a basic level required to develop artisanal skills) he did lay the foundations for modern Sudanese education. From no money to teach at all in 1900 to a budget of £58,057 in 1913, and from virtually no formal schooling to around six thousand boys being educated, was an achievement. Gordon College went from primary schooling to having laboratories and facilities for training teachers and surveyors. Currie was knighted and given a government post in Sudan, and decorated by the Khedive of Egypt. Like other Old Fettesians, typical men of their era and background in their attitudes, Currie had, as Mangan puts it, a 'narrow and decent ambition'[33] which could have been a lot worse.

4. Fettesians in the Army

An enormous number of Fettesians joined the army: between 1870 and 1900, 1509 boys passed through the school; 207 (14%) became professional soldiers. This is not counting those who joined colonial militias as imperial civil servants or settlers, or those who served in county volunteers or territorials at home; there was a burst of volunteering during the Boer War which saw both those in the United Kingdom and their contemporaries in Canada and Australia flock to the colours of local units. If it did, the proportion of Old Fettesians with some sort of military experience before the outbreak of the First World War would be at least a quarter.

If the Victorian public schools were changing in order to produce a more intellectually, physically, and morally healthy alumnus than the gentleman thug of yesteryear, so too the army was, sometimes reluctantly, modernizing. Indeed, it can be argued that much of what we know of the British army today dates from the late Victorian era, whether its full-dress uniforms, regimental structure or obsession with all forms of sport (rather than just gambling and hunting, as was the case in earlier times).[34] The reforms were chiefly associated with Gladstone's gifted Secretary of State for War, Edward Cardwell, though some had begun in the 1850s as a result of the Crimean War. Fettes master John Beith, better known as the writer Ian Hay, saw Cardwell as the father of the modern British Army which he and his fellow Fettesians would serve with such loyalty; before Cardwell, he wrote, 'chaos reigned supreme', and it was 'signal proof of the man's greatness' that he achieved his ambitious twin goals of professionalizing the Army and putting it under rational, homogenous, democratic control.[35]

Cardwell changed the terms of service from twenty-one years to three, with nine in the reserve, on the European model, and gave permanent homes to regiments in the hope that this would create organic bonds of local pride between soldiers and society. He transferred control of county militias from the lords-lieutenant to central government and brought the Horse Guards under clearer political control. Most importantly, in 1871 his Army Regulations Bill abolished the purchase of commissions, so that 'the officers must belong to the Army, and not the Army to the officers'[36] – an important reform which would benefited middle-class Fettesians, but which was vigorously opposed by traditionalists.

The Old Fettesian who entered the army in the late nineteenth century was joining a force which was undoubtedly more popular in terms of public esteem than it had been before, even if huge sections of the public were still unwilling to take their jingoistic support so far as to actually join it, and one which was groping its way towards greater professionalism. Sandhurst and, in particular, Woolwich (where the artillery and engineer officers were trained) were becoming more technical in their training. The great public schools, Fettes included, eventually ran an Army Class for sixth-formers keen to get a commission, in which classicists might learn the rudiments of science so as to cope with this.

The first ever issue of the *Fettesian* magazine in 1878 recorded that Hutchinson, Lenox-Conyngham and Swinton were at Sandhurst, whilst Cook had already passed out and gained a staff appointment in India. The author of an early letter from Sandhurst to Fettes hoped that 'lots more Fettesians will come here as the times go on', but did point to a key reason why, despite the abolition of purchasing commissions, the officer ranks remained closed to people of working-class origins:

Pay consists of 3s. per diem (one never sees it), and one's outlay for the same period is 3s. 11d. [for food and laundry]... For the year that one is here one pays £125 in two sums of £62, 10s., one at the beginning of each term, and also at the beginning one pays £25 for uniform and £5 contingent...

The average wage for a skilled worker was £62 per annum, which ensured that no such people would disturb the respectable atmosphere of the officers' mess. This would not have been considered in any way odd to the Victorian mind; everything, it was reasoned, needed to be paid for, and a chap who couldn't pay his way had no right to want to be an officer.

Virtually every issue of the school magazine from its first appearance up to the outbreak of war in 1914 had some reference to old boys who entered Sandhurst or Woolwich, and others who were on active service. This announcement will stand for all the others:

The following have appeared in recent Gazettes:- The Suffolk Regiment – Lieut. F.P. Hutchinson (O.F.) 1st Batn., a probationer, officiating squadron-officer, 19th Bengal N.I., is about to be admitted to the Staff Corps, with effect from August 5, 1880. The Gordon Highlanders – Gent. Cadet R.S. Hunter-Blair (O.F.) from Sandhurst, to be Lieutenant. The Sherwood Foresters – Gent. Cadet T.G. Gordon-Cumming from the R.M.C., to be Lieutenant. Both commissions dated October 22, 1881.

The same number also carried news of Lieutenants James Hope and Walter Cook, who had been decorated, J. Rutherford-Clark, W.D. Sellar and D.A. M'Leod, who had entered Sandhurst, and R.S. Hunter-Blair and L.S. Gordon-Cumming, who had passed out of it. The sheer tide of such information forced the *Fettesian* to start printing formal Army Lists from March 1882, when 17 names appeared in full-time service – a remarkable total for a school of less than a hundred boys which had only been open for ten years. Within ten years there would be over 60, plus three surgeons and five retired soldiers. These people often kept in touch with their old school. 'A Recruit' wrote to describe life in training:

For an hour we are doomed to sit and listen to the attempts of a professor to impress upon our imaginations the different peculiarities of the missiles used for smooth-bore and rifled ordnance, etc... we have exercised our arms, we have done our best to develop our chests, and the next part of the setting-up process is dedicated to the acquirement of that erect and soldier-like bearing, the beloved of every colonel in its acquisition, the abhorred of every recruit...

From 10.25 until 2 there is little variation – tactics and fortifications, fortifications and tactics... Little time is given for relaxation; half-an-hour to scramble through some luncheon, and the bugle once more rings out its summons, and we have to tumble out and parade until three, unless it happens to be a gymnastic day...

The light-heartedness of this approach was often criticized by the public; despite Cardwell's best efforts, there were no grand organized field exercises, planning remained limited, and there was still a general dislike of lectures. However, as at school, sport often filled a gap left by the academic side, encouraging teamwork and fitness. Another former pupil at Sandhurst saw this side of life as a major attraction of an army career:

The life suits anyone who is at all manly, and consequently would suit most of the rising generation, shall I say? Of amusements there is no lack: football and cricket in their respective seasons, tennis... The Staff College hounds, and sundry packs of beagles, are always on hand if one wants a run.

Lewis Robertson, a Fettesian rugby international who played for Monkstown in Ireland, Edinburgh Wanderers, United Services and (of course) both London Scottish and Fettesian-Lorettonian, 'found ample scope for the exercise of his keenness on games and athletic pursuits, being especially keen on gymnastics and bayonet fighting.'[37] A contemporary described him as:

Quite the hardest man to ever come up against I ever met on the football field. He used to go through every game with teeth clenched, often muttering to himself to spur him on. He was a terror to run up against, as hard as a nail and a fighter through and through, until he was absolutely stopped.[38]

The Fettes gymnastics team of 1894 with 'Sarge' Adam, the Scots Guards Crimean War veteran who taught physical education and drill from 1874 until 1911. Three of these athletes went on to be highly-decorated soldiers. Note 'apprentice pillar' on the left, inspired by Rosslyn Chapel

When war broke out in 1914, the Scottish Rugby Football Union declared that the sport was ideal training for a fighting man, encouraging as it did quick decision-making, dash, and, oddly, 'self-restraint and consideration for opponents.' Against this notion of sport in general and Fettesian rugby in particular as vital in building a warrior caste, it should be noted that neither Donald Mackintosh nor Bertie Anderson, the school's two Victoria Cross winners of 1914-18, were especially good at games.

Once in the army (less than a dozen joined the navy), former pupils continued to write back about their adventures. Naturally, these included sport, and the school rejoiced when its old boys won military competitions A 'griff' (junior officer) in India wrote to the school describing the sport which could be enjoyed on leave, including 'the king of sports – pigsticking':

The first pig broke near our party, and, after giving it sufficient law, we gave chase. My pony dashed off, and we were soon close behind the boar, who, of course, then changed his course. I, however, didn't – or rather couldn't – and when I managed to stop my beast the pig was its death throes. Shortly afterwards another broke out at the same place, and the same performance was gone through.

As we charged wildly on I saw a herd of water buffaloes loom large in the distance, and, though I had no say in the matter, thought that my mare could not be such a fool as not to avoid them. However, she didn't, and we cannoned into one with a crash which nearly made us part company. This rather steadied down my wild steed, and I managed to turn her in the direction of the others, who were closely following the pig, and then let her rip. As we came up to them at an angle the pig saw us and turned in to take us sideways. I put down my spear, onto which piggy ran, and then I went on. When we again joined the party the boar was laid out at the feet of the others, and I was informed it was mine. I trust I bore the unexpected honour with becoming modesty.

The letters from active service gave at least some insight into the rigours of army life. George Dillon sent his first dispatch from Burma in 1886, apologizing in advance that it would savour of what his 'compositions used to be at Fettes, baldness':

You at home in luxury do not know what 'rain' means out here; if you want to find out, get a man to turn a garden pump

*on you for six hours or so without cessation, and even then you
don't approach it. Our journey here was not very pleasant –
1000 miles by rail to Calcutta, 1000 miles by sea thence to
Rangoon, and another 1000 miles by river up the Irrawaddy to
here. I suppose I ought to write volumes on the subject of the
ever-varying scenery coming up the river, but, as a matter of
fact, the scenery on either bank was just about as tame as you
could see; nothing wild about it at all...*

*I thought India had taught me what a mosquito was, but
to see mosquitos as large as snipe and in coveys you must come
to Burmah. Any man under twelve stone is lifted from his bed
and mangled without the slightest difficulty. I have made a vow
to despise the midge of England when I have the luck to meet
him.*

Dillon had been sent to the area 'with instructions to kill
and slay' the gangs of murderous dacoits (robbers) which
supposedly infested it. He ended up marching around over
'fiendish country', covering 37 miles in 48 hours, but ended up
only arresting a few 'gentlemen'. A subsequent experience of
battle when his company and another tried to seize some
mountain stockades led to some rueful observations:

*That it was pretty hot work you may gather from the fact
that, out of six officers under fire, three were wounded (two
severely) as well as nine men. The sensation of being 'under fire'
is very funny, and not as pleasant as it might be; these fellows
creep up pretty close in the jungle and let fly with a muzzle-
loader crammed with slugs as big as your fist, and which make
a hole you could put your head in.*

In a subsequent report, he described the emotions of battle
– 'I had a sort of funny feeling in the pit of my stomach until I
caught sight of one of them, and then one hadn't time to bother
much; besides, I got a wee bit bloodthirsty.' Dillon himself
survived four campaigns and was awarded both medals and
clasps, was mentioned in dispatches three times and was
awarded the C.B. in 1903, but died of illness at sea in 1906.

The numbers and activity of Fettesians overseas can be
seen in the school magazine's announcements pages. To take just
one example, in December 1892, news included the death from
typhoid at Poona on 15 August of Lt. Henry Simson, 'an
exceedingly smart officer' who had been a member of the school
cricket XI. A.G.H. Carruthers, serving in China, had 'evidently

lost none of his old skill and cunning' on the pitch, helping Shanghai defeat Hong Kong in the interport cricket match – an event overshadowed by tragedy when the returning Hong Kong players were lost with the SS *Bokhara*, which sank in a typhoon. On 14 November at Rangoon, Carruthers' brother Robert, an officer in the Bengal Lancers seconded to the Burmese Military Police, married Miss Florence Wintle; he would later captain the Military Police polo team and the Rangoon, all-Burma and Police cricket teams against a visiting side from Ceylon, and was an accomplished practitioner of the equestrian art of tent-pegging, winning championships in Rangoon and Mandalay. (It was, incidentally, one of these Carruthers who had taken part in the vertical raid on the school larder in the 1870s – Fettes' preparation for military derring-do was not confined to officially-sanctioned sport and moral exhortation.) On 12 December, Lt. Cecil Mitchell-Innes, stationed in Pachmari, became a proud father (he later became Chief Constable of Lincolnshire). Imperial life was undoubtedly crowded for OFs.

5. The North-West Frontier

India had been more or less subdued by the time Fettes was opened, but the North-West Frontier with Afghanistan was a running sore for a host of reasons. The tribes of the region were aggressive, occasionally prone to becoming over-excited by some new Islamist prophet, and relaxed about raiding the lands of the Indian farmers they despised. Afghanistan was also a potential route for the Tsar into India, and Russian invasion was a constant fear of the Victorians. At least a dozen Old Fettesians served with distinction on the Frontier, and others were involved in administration, medicine or education in surrounding provinces. These were often prolific letter-writers. The third issue of the school magazine carried a detailed account from 'Piffer' (the nickname for soldiers of the Punjab Frontier Force) of a day's march:

We are obliged to march early in order to avoid the noonday heat; so the 'Révaillé' sounds at 2.30am and in a few minutes every one is up and awake, the camp echoing with a medley of sounds, camels groaning, as only camels can, mules braying, and men chattering as they strike their tents, for Jack Sepoy is a tremendous fellow to talk even at 3 o'clock in the morning... so 'quick march' off we go, tramp tramp to the skirl of the bagpipes; for, O incredulous Scot, the gallant – Punjab Infantry does boast of bagpipes and stalwart pipers too, albeit they may be a shade darker than their Teutonic brethren, Dougal and Donald of the 42nd!
We step along merrily, for the morning is sharp and cold, although the sun will be hot enough in an hour or two, and the men soon settle down into their long swinging step which, although less regular than British marching, yet takes them along at about four miles per hour. But now the morning star has risen and soon the rising sun gilds the snow-clad peaks of the lower Himalayas, some hundred miles to our right, while to our left the morning mist rises ghost-like from the broad Indus. The air grows sharper just as the sun tops the horizon, but the men step out more freely, now they can see where to tread...

The romance and enthusiasm of this is unlikely to have been lost on the young readers back at Fettes. The following year

'Piffer' wrote from the Khyber Pass, where he was taking part in an attack on the fortress of Ali Musjid:

> *In the grey dawn, as our men are eagerly scanning the long defile which now lies at their feet, a body of the enemy's cavalry, some 200 strong, appears round a corner of the Pass, in retreat from Ali Musjid. A couple of shots brings them to a halt, and their leader motions them to retire where an intervening rock gives safe cover from our fire. They have only two courses open to them to follow, one is to at once surrender, the other to run the gauntlet of our fire up the Pass. Their leader, brave fellow that he is, prefers the latter. Dashing forward, he fires his pistol, and at the signal the whole troop put spurs to their horses and gallop madly up the Pass. A sharp fire is poured into them, and many a good horse and bold rider falls struggling on the fast reddening stones...*

'Piffer' was the pseudonym of Walter Cook, one of seven 'patriarchs' to join the army. He was later reported to have 'greatly distinguished himself in the defence of the Shutargardan position'; he was wounded but 'thanks to a stoutish rib, the ball fell out again' as his letter put it. The enemy positions were well entrenched on a rocky ridge, the approach to which was 'difficult and almost precipitous, affording scarcely any cover' and could only be taken in a coordinated attack from two sides. To organize this, Cook, on the right of the hill, ran 200 yards under heavy fire to the 21st Punjabis on the left, and, when his senior officer was hit, also went to get help, despite even heavier fire. Cook could have ordered one of his men to take a note to the Punjabis or to the dooly-wallahs (stretcher-bearers), but felt it would be better if he could explain the situation in person.

Both he and his brother John were severely wounded at Kabul in December 1879; fighting shoulder to shoulder, they led a bayonet charge in a counter-attack against a 'persistent and bold' Afghan force, and both were shot. John lay wounded in the open overnight, and when told that the operation to amputate his leg would kill him, he simply said 'Dulce et decorum est pro Patria mori', which Walter, writing home, described as the normal observation of a soldier.

Recommended for the Victoria Cross, Walter Cook's career was followed by admiring friends; a letter from an OF in Calcutta in 1881 said Cook was on Roberts' march to Kandahar, when he had his horse shot from under him, and was subsequently stationed in a small frontier station in the Punjab; by 1887 he was taking command of a force of police in what was then called Burmah. By the time of his retirement he was commanding officer of the 43rd Gurkhas; he returned to Scotland and lived to be almost ninety.

When war returned to the North-West Frontier in the 1890s – it was never far away – an un-named OF wrote, at the request of the Headmaster, to explain what was happening there as the British attempted to fight the fiery Mahsud Waziris.

Month after month stories of looted caravans, burnt villages, women and children carried off, were brought to the authorities; the marauders were chased, but with little effect, as they escaped across the frontier, and policy demanded that we should not cross this frontier, as the Amir of Kabul was very apt to take umbrage at any infringement of his territory under any circumstances. The Waziris, however, neither acknowledged the Amir nor the British, so that, with very few exceptions, the marauders escaped without punishment.

...In the autumn of 1894 the British party started, marching into Waziristan accompanied by a strong escort of troops to meet the Afghan representatives. For a time all went well; the Waziris gave no trouble, assisted in procuring supplies for the force, for which they were paid, and appeared to be on the most friendly terms.

On the 4th November, however, the British camp was rushed just before daybreak by 2000 or 3000 Waziris, who got into the camp and killed a certain number of men, followers, and animals. The countryside was in a blaze, the mullahs or priests preaching religious war on the so-called invaders of their territory, signal fires on every mountaintop calling all the young men to arms, and matters looked very serious.

The author, who felt that the British had been 'too long-suffering' in the face of Waziri marauding in the past, had been 'hoping, without any hope' that he would be asked to join the punitive force which was drawn up to overrun Waziristan and teach the 'young bloods' to behave. He was delighted to receive a telegram appointing him Deputy-Assistant Adjutant-General to the 3rd Brigade, and made a three-day train journey and 80-mile trip in a cart from his base at Quetta in Baluchistan to Bannu, where he was immediately set to work organizing the fitting out of the force with fifteen days' rations for 2,500 fighting men, plus their followers, 1,800 camels and 1,000 mules. Horses were of little use in the high mountains, so they marched for 12 to 14 miles a day, spending Christmas Eve bivouacking at 8,000 feet without tents, sending out flying columns to punish offending villages by seizing their cattle and destroying their defences. The Waziris were related to the Pathans, who the author commanded and admired, so he was able to gain a little insight into their way of life:

The tribe is estimated at about 12,000 fighting men, principally armed with swords and matchlocks, though of late a good many rifles have found their way into the country. They make their own swords, and beautiful weapons some of them are (we came across numberless smelting places on the hills, which abound with iron). They are all thieves, and proud of being so, and personally brave.

Men and women alike are addicted to tobacco chewing, but none drink intoxicating drinks. Their food consists mainly of wheat, Indian corn, rice, and barley, which they grow themselves. Hospitality is a prime virtue amongst them and the life of a guest is safe so long as he is within the precincts of the village. There are no doctors or physicians, the usual and only treatment of a practical nature being to roll the patient in a sheepskin for twelve hours; but they mostly rely on charms and incantations...

They are very ignorant, and as a sure result very fanatical, trusting themselves entirely to their priest. Every village and every homestead a strong stone tower into which they retire when attacked. This goes far to show the pleasant terms on which they live with each other.

An Old Fettesian sent a cutting from the *Daily Graphic* to the school which described his contemporary Donald Watt's work at Malakand:

At eleven o'clock the main attack was made on Malakand by the Scottish Borderers and Gordon Highlanders. The enemy disputed every inch of ground, but after four hours' fighting the position was carried by the two regiments with great gallantry. Second Lieutenant Watt, of the Kings' Own Scottish Borderers, was the first to reach the summit. Thinking his men were close behind him and he rushed at a 'sangar', out of which three of the enemy came to meet him. These he promptly shot with his revolver, upon which more of the tribesmen came out. Lieutenant Watt, finding himself alone, turned back to his men, who at that moment came over the crest. The sangar was then carried by storm.

'Fettes leads the way in India as well as in Scotland,' crowed the former pupil, 'may she ever do so!' A letter from Watt (who was actually in the Gordons), published a few months later, pointed out that much of the really important work at the battle had been done by Sergeant Ewan from Banffshire, who 'killed any amount' of tribesmen with the Maxim machine-gun: Watt was pleased that the K.O.S.B. afterwards said that they could not have advanced without this. Of his own exploits, he was rather matter-of-fact:

To the left the way was easy, but we could not advance owing to the heavy fire of the enemy; to the right it was like going up a rope, pulling yourself up by means of grass tufts and cracks in the rocks. Whoever started first would be up first. As I was afraid of the K.O.S.B.s getting up first I started off, telling the nearest men to follow. At the top there was a tree, and I got under cover of this and had a look round. There was a house about 4yds. or so from it, and I saw several 'nigs,' but presently they all disappeared. Then I went towards the house, shouting to the men to come up. They had been too beat to follow me. My shouting at once brought three 'nigs' from the other side of the house. I killed two and wounded the third with my revolver, and then went and looked down both sides of the spur, but not a soul was coming up, so I went back and found five or six of the enemy, and any amount behind them making for me. So I let fly at them with my revolver.

Then I had another look, and seeing more coming up I sat and slid down the hill back to the 'sungar.' I went down the exposed side, as the other was too steep to get down quickly without going to the bottom of the hill. On the way, my sword fell out of the sheath and ran into my leg; it went in the front of my thigh and came out just where the leg joins the body, making two holes about 4in. apart. It got caught in a bush and so was pulled out; I picked it up and got into the 'sungar.' The enemy had been firing and chucking stones at me, so I got the first men I met in the 'sungar' to come to the left corner of it and answer their fire. The first was a corporal in the K.O.S.B, and just as he was going to aim he fell dead down the hill, and I got at the same moment the most awful smack on the left shoulder. A bullet had cut the shoulder strap, scored the leather strap of

my revolver case, and cut my coat behind the shoulder. It made
me jump a bit.

Watt rose to the rank of Brigadier-General, commanding
officer of the 5th Gurkhas, serving in Afghanistan and in the First
World War. The journalist Henry Hamilton Fyfe, one of his
contemporaries, later recalled that as a boy, Watt was discussing
with some other pupils what they would become. One was to be a
lawyer, another was destined for medicine, a third for a family
business, and so on. Watt kept silence until all the rest had
spoken, then said solemnly, 'Ah'm goin to be a ma-an'. 'He kept
his word,' wrote Hamilton Fyfe.

Watt survived a series of wars more or less intact. Others
were less fortunate. Major E.W.M. Norie of the Gurkha Rifles,
however, was so badly injured by a dum-dum bullet in the Bara
Valley that his arm had to be amputated. On 17 August 1897,
Hector Lachlan Stewart MacLean of the Corps of Guides was
killed trying, 'under a very heavy and close fire', to save a
wounded comrade from enemy swordsmen at Nawa Kili, Upper
Swat. Winston Churchill, in *The Story of the Malakand Field
Force*, described MacLean's earlier 'wonderful escape', when 'a
bullet entered his mouth and passed through his cheek without
injuring the bone in any way.'[39] Churchill and many others felt
that MacLean deserved the highest award for gallantry, and
when Edward VII decided posthumously to honour those whose
bravery would have earned them decorations had they survived,
he did indeed receive the Victoria Cross.

The *Fettesian* carried a glowing tribute from former Head
of School, Alfred Hamilton Grant of the Indian Civil Service, who
wrote to the school that MacLean 'was one of the most popular
men in one of the most popular regiments in India, and was
renowned as one of the finest polo-players in the Punjab.' Grant
also sent the school a poem in honour of his friend:

Hold fast your tears: it is not meet to weep.
Tears are the meed of deaths that, incomplete,
Cut down the flower, ere yet the hue doth peep
From out the velvet bulb's sheath. Tears are meet
For shipwreck'd lives, and deaths that bring an end
To barren hopes, to want, disease, to shame.
So hold your tears. For he, MacLean, your friend,
Died not as frost-nipp'd bud, an empty name,
Nor yet in hopes unfruitful; want, disease,
Or shame had never sullied the fair page

Of that brave, vigorous life. From tears then cease.
E'en the wild foe to wonder turn'd from rage,
As, self-forgetful, on to Death he hurl'd –
True to his corps, a Guide to all the world.

Lt. Hector MacLean, VC
(Picture supplied by the Clan Maclean Heritage Trust)

Most of the Fettesians regarded violent death as a price worth paying occasionally for what Dillon called 'a rather jolly posting' but there were still other, more permanent risks. Chief among these was disease, which killed well over half of the military and colonial Old Fettesians who died before the outbreak of the First World War. In November 1898, for instance, Archibald Hepburne-Michelson in Singapore and Edward Boyle in Malta were recorded as having died young; typhoid or enteric fever were the usual culprits. Accidents claimed many: Lt. A.S. Stephen slipped on the steps of his bungalow in Ranjapur and broke his spine. He doggedly dragged himself onto a horse and rode thirty miles, but had to be taken back home to die. Two fellow Old Fettesians, serving with the 5th Punjab Cavalry, were among the pallbearers.

Former pupils of Fettes took part in military operations on the North-West Frontier (known to British soldiers as 'the grim') up to, during, and after the Great War. On 10 May 1917, 27-year-old Capt. Francis Charteris Davidson of the South Waziristan Militia, a former prizewinning classical scholarship boy, school prefect and athlete, was killed by attacking Mahsuds at Sarwekai on the Mohmand border. His name appears on a plaque in Haddington parish church and on the school war memorial alongside his comrades who died on the Western Front; buried in a remote scout post, his grave has now been lost.

6. Wild Colonial Boys

It has to be admitted also that not all of the Fettesians overseas were brave warriors or high-minded missionaries, teachers or administrators. Plenty went overseas in search of profit and were indifferent to the locals' well-being. A letter from the Ceylon highlands in 1879 was fairly frank about the tea-planter's life:

> The coolies have to turn out every morning at six o'clock to muster, wet or dry, and so have the 'Sinna Dorés' or 'young sirs'; the 'Peria Dorés' or 'big sirs' staying in their bungalows or in their beds according to their inclinations, and only coming out when they want to do or say something particular, or occasionally to catch a coolie sleeping in a drain when he ought to be at work cutting it, or perhaps to catch the Sinna Dorés playing pranks, instead of looking after the coolies.
>
> The Europeans of course enjoy this cool weather and snap their fingers at the rain; but it is altogether a different matter with the coolies. Thinly clad in cotton cloth, which gets immediately wet, they look the very pictures of misery, and although the estate provides them with 'Cambulies', a sort of thin blanket which they wear over their heads and shoulders, their shivering forms and loud complaints as they work away all show how much they feel the change in the weather.

The author was also breezily honest about working practices on the plantations:

> A Kanganie is a sort of a head man who has a few coolies under him, and is told off to drive a lot in such and such a work, the which he accomplishes by means of a stout stick, and he is no mean hand in wielding it, and loud are the howls and execrations one hears sometimes, attesting both to their power of arm, volubility of tongue, and fertility of imagination. At any rate the Kangani gets 'nailed' by the Sinna Doré if anything is wrong in his work so he has to adopt the maxim of 'spare the rod and spoil the child.'

That he did not feel any need to keep quiet about such matters says much about the assumptions of the time. Like many

OFs abroad, the author was keen to encourage his successors to come out and give this opportunity a try:

> *Planting is a rough life, and one must means be no carpet-knight to succeed well in it. But although it has its fatigues, and to a beginner they are somewhat formidable, yet the life is active, and plenty of fun can be got from it...*

Another glimpse of the Empire's less savoury aspects was provided by Robert Bruce Lockhart, who, before his days as a diplomat, made an unsuccessful attempt to increase the family fortune in the Far East. Unlike some other OFs, he did not flinch from describing the sordid underside of colonial life, notably in his various memoirs, written in the thirties. He remembered Madame Blanche's 'frail army of white women recruited by the professional pimps from the poorest population of Central and Eastern Europe.'[40] No British girls, of course – the authorities did not allow this on political grounds, lest the dignity of the imperium be called into question by a local chap hoping to satisfy 'an exotic and perhaps politically perverted desire for the embraces of the forbidden white women.' The bulk of the prostitutes were bought from poor Japanese families by local 'contractors' who brought them to Malaya to service the thousands of Chinese coolies in the mines; they were to all intents slaves.

Although Lockhart wrote that 'this traffic in human souls had roused in me feelings of resentment both against the Japanese and against the existing social order' and that 'in my moods of reflection I had been disgusted by this cruel and senseless wastage of human life,' he admitted to lapses on his own part; his antics with other young Britons were certainly not the sort of thing Fettes wished to encourage among its alumni. After football matches, he had taken part in 'jollifications' with other young expatriates which involved copious drinking, boisterous horseplay, ribald songs and visits to brothels. On quieter, more private occasions, he had 'driven down the street furtively, with the hood of the ricksha up, afraid lest any pair of eyes behind the shuttered windows were witnesses to the white man's secret shame.'

Lockhart wrote this description of Singapore's seedy delights and hidden horrors in 1936, by which time the drive of the imperialists for improvement had largely eradicated the vice trade, or at least its most obvious and pernicious manifestations, and provided – predictably – a vast array of sports facilities in which young Britons might work off their excess energy in a healthier fashion. In 1906, however, Lockhart saw the challenge of going 'up-country' as the way to break free from the expatriate cycle of drunken debauchery, and was sent to open up a new plantation in an inhospitable area with an unenviable death-rate from malaria: 'I had to make something out of nothing, an estate out of jungle, to build a house for myself, to make roads and drains where none existed.'[41]

He was able to gain the respect of the locals by shooting a cobra which had made its home in the local well with a single, and rather lucky, bullet to the head. This gave the locals the impression that he always carried a revolver and was a crack shot, so he was not molested by troublemakers. Nonetheless, his midnight rides through ten miles of jungle, most of which was uninhabited, on his bicycle were a special kind of thrill.

After six months living apart from other Britons, and a whole year apart from white women, the 23-year-old Lockhart noted that 'steeped in an unhealthy romanticism, I was ripe for temptation', which came in the form of Amai, the dazzlingly beautiful ward of the local sultan. Despite being warned by his Malay headman that 'the crow does not mate with the bird of paradise' and by the Irish colonial police commissioner that since native women all looked the same anyway he ought to go for others more easily attainable and less dangerous, Bruce Lockhart arranged secret meetings with Amai, who moved into his bungalow. This caused a scandal in Malay society; whilst the British may have believed themselves to be superior, so far as the local aristocracy was concerned this was a mere tradesman who had made off with a princess. An Anglophile footballing prince tried to talk Lockhart round over stengahs, but he stood his ground, claiming that he was ready to convert to 'Mohammedanism' if necessary. Malay friends and staff melted away and Lockhart developed malaria; when his uncle heard of it, he sent a car and bundled the enfeebled romantic into it, then onto a ship, where he gradually recovered his health whilst pining for his beloved and writing bad poetry.

Will Ogilvie, by contrast, was known for his good poetry. After leaving Fettes in 1888, he worked initially on his family's land at Kelso, but spent twelve years roaming around the Australian bush as a stockman and horse-breaker. Ogilvie's flair for poetry had been noticed at Fettes, where he won a prize for it, but his passion for the wonders of the outback made him beloved in Australia. His entry in the *Australian Dictionary of Biography* eulogises the way that 'his rhythmic lines seem to keep time to the beat of horse-hooves, the crack of the stockwhip and the clink of snaffle-bars.'[42]

In 1893 Ogilvie wrote a poem for the *Fettesian* which encapsulates both the excitement of Empire and the love of the old school which inspired so many of the former pupils in the nineteenth century (not to mention the pervasive influence of Longfellow's 'Hiawatha'). It was written on the back of a copy of the school magazine as Ogilvie sat at the foot of a gum tree, and reflects both the excitement of settler life and the Fettesian devotion to school:

I am writing from Australia,
From the land of gold and gum trees,
Writing to my younger brothers
In the land of fight and fives-balls
In the land where snowy fives-balls
Leap way above the side walls
To the thieving roofs, and stay there.

Here we hunt the brown opossum
From his home among the treetops,
In the moonlight from the treetops
Drop him with the double barrel;
Take his skin as prize and trophy,
Weave it into rugs for winter
For our friends in far-off Scotland.
Here we mount our steed at morning,
In the golden South-land morning,
Gallop out among the ranges,
Follow from the rocky ranges
Where the kangaroo, the brusher,
Leads the chase across the hollows,
Spur the good horse up beside him,
Stun him with the stirrup-iron –
Make his skin a wrap for winter...

So we toil or take our pleasure
In the Sun-land, in Australia,
In the very great Australia;
But we sometimes grow aweary,
And our hearts are sore within us
For the good old days in Scotland,
For the merry days at Fettes.
And we sometimes hear in sleeping

All the Fettes bells at morning:
First bell – second bell – at morning,
And we sometimes hear the last bell –
Very cruel was the last bell –
And we hear at times the cheering
Coming from the crowded touch lines,
When we battle with Loretto,
With the scarlet of Loretto,
When the feet are thundering goalwards
Like the roar of battle squadrons
In a dribble of the forwards.
And we sometimes see in dreaming
All the corridors of Fettes
Thronged with many laughing fellows
Rushing to their different classrooms
When the bell is nearly stopping.
And we wake, and are not happy,
For those merry days are over,
All the fun and laugh is over.
Is it strange we love our masters,
Love our tutors and form-masters?
And our merry, merry comrades –
Is it strange that we should love them?

Golden through the gum tree branches
In its splendour glows the sunset,
And I canter slowly homewards –
No! I am not late for lockup –
But my heart is sad for Fettes.[43]

Despite the absence of armed enemies in these corners of the Empire, danger still lurked; the school learned in 1895 that Fred Marshall, a popular member of the 1889 1st XV, had died far from home. 'A boy of splendid physique', although 'intellectually he did not take a high place', he had studied at a colonial college to prepare for life as a 'sturdy squatter' in New Zealand:

His death was sad, and characteristic of the boy. Seized with illness some distance out in the bush when almost alone, he started to ride home. As he rode on over the rough track he found himself getting weaker, till it last he could ride no longer. But he gamely struggled on on foot, and literally crawling the last few miles of the way, he got home just in time to die.

Patriarch Henry Holmes Gallie accidentally shot himself whilst looking for a tiger in the middle of the night on a tea plantation in Upper Assam on 26 October 1882. George Horan was only nineteen when he perished in the wreck of the SS *Tararua* in 1881. The ship was sailing from Dunedin to Melbourne when it became stuck on a reef at Waipapa point and was gradually smashed by the waves with the loss of over a hundred passengers and crew. A contemporary newspaper report recorded that Horan was a good scholar 'but the sea had a peculiar charm for him, like many other young men.' It was only his second voyage.[44] Shipwreck also claimed the life of Duncan Buchanan, freshly posted to Bermuda with the Leinster Regiment, drowned aged twenty-two when the sailing-boat *Juno* sank in a squall en route from Hamilton to Agar's Island. Indeed, along with disease, drowning seems to have been a common fate for the Fettesian imperialist, with at least half a dozen lost this way before the Great War broke out. Two ranchers were killed by lightning strikes, one in Argentina and the other in South Africa. The Fettes boy of the late nineteenth and early twentieth centuries might have been protected from the squalor of Britain's industrial slums, but he can surely have had no illusions about the toughness of life.

The wreck of the Tararua, *in which former pupil George Horan was lost*

7. Reports from Africa

Despite the physical and moral dangers of all the many global postings Victorian Fettesians might experience, it was Africa that was to see the largest number killed before the outbreak of the First World War. As in India, the Fettesian presence was a combination of military, administrative and commercial, with both idealism and business ambitions represented.

Lewis Wroughton, for instance, joined the Basutoland service in 1884 as a Sub-Inspector of the Police and had completed 28 years of 'good and faithful service' when he succumbed to illness in 1912. By the time of his death he was Acting Resident Commissioner at Maseru and in this role produced the annual report on the territory for Parliament. This documented the successes of British rule, including an increase in the number of children being educated (15,397, an increase of over two thousand since the previous year), electric light for the Maseru hospital, and new bridges at Mohale's Hoek, Leriba and Berea. Between 1910 and 1912 the number of postage stamps being sold had gone up by £269 6s. 8d. and £21,441 in postal orders had been issued. The Basutoland Council, composed of 99 representatives of the local chiefs, worked only too well:

The point that would probably strike a visitor is the courtesy and politeness with which members treat each other, as well as the moderate tone of the speeches made in the course of the debate. It would seem that nervousness is the product of civilisation, for in this council, whose members have only comparatively recently come into contact with European forms and procedure, every member speaks fluently and easily, and it is practically unknown for a member to stammer, hesitate, or repeat himself unconsciously. The principal fault to be found with the debates is their tendency to drag on to undue lengths...[45]

Not all was so successful; heavy rains had harmed the crops, there were persistent reports of brandy smuggling (public opinion, though opposed to alcohol, was 'not sufficiently strong to induce the people to side actively with the government in suppressing it'), and a native had murdered a relative in cold blood. On the whole, though, Wroughton's last report was upbeat. The High Commissioner for Southern Africa, Herbert Gladstone (son of the Victorian statesman) had visited to proclaim George V as the new king, and this had gone extremely well. Met at the station by the Paramount Chief and 20,000 mounted natives, His Excellency had reviewed the troops at the racecourse and held a Pitso (grand public meeting) at which he heard declarations of loyalty from local dignitaries. His reply advised the Basuto 'to be law abiding and obedient to the officers over them, to refrain from using firearms in their disputes, and generally to merit the protection which had been so long extended to them by His Majesty's Government.' This had a 'great effect' and the meeting dispersed to happy shouts of 'peace' and 'rain'. Such was the life of a Fettesian colonial official in Africa during peacetime.

Africa was to see Fettes' first war casualty, on 22 January 1879. James Adrian Blaikie, aged nineteen, was an amiable-looking young man with wispy whiskers. His family had emigrated from Aberdeen to Pietermaritzburg when he was ten, but he was sent back to Scotland 'to complete his education' in 1873. He returned to the Natal Colony and was working in a solicitor's office when he joined the Natal Carbineers, possibly at the suggestion of George Shepstone, a widely-respected local lawyer who was, like Blaikie, his commander Lt. Frederick Scott, and a number of other troopers, a former pupil of the local high school. The Carbineers were part of a British force led by Lord Chelmsford which had advanced into Zululand to teach King Cetshwayo a lesson.

Unfortunately, a series of errors led the British camp at Isandlwana, ill-defended and loaded down with heavy equipment, to be attacked by twenty thousand Zulu warriors. The Zulus' overwhelming numbers and concentrated attack strategy, and some confusion on the part of the British (including, according to some accounts, the inability to open ammunition boxes in time) led to the destruction of Chelmsford's column.

The Natal Carbineers had made a heroic last stand with Lt.-Col. Anthony Durnford, a senior officer they apparently disliked because he had accused them of cowardice after an incident at Bushman's River Pass. For Blaikie and Scott, this might have had a personal element, since another former pupil of Pietermaritzburg High School, Robert Erskine, had been killed there. Yet when Durnford, realizing that all was lost, shouted 'Now, my men, let us see what you can do!' they rallied to him. Saul David remarks that 'they were all excellent horsemen and crack shots, and could easily have escaped as a group, yet incredibly they chose a hero's death.' A Zulu witness recalled that they fought shoulder to shoulder, and back to back, until their ammunition was exhausted, then carried on with their knives to the last man.[46] Their sacrifice temporarily blocked the wagon road to Natal and enabled a small number of survivors to escape. The school's obituary recorded that:

> *Little is known of his end. Muirhead, the only carbineer who escaped, reported that he died nobly, cool and steady, and encouraging the men to the end. He and Lieutenant Scott were together; they both kept their heads throughout, though some of their comrades fainted. We may judge of the horrors of the field, when we are told that the greatest comfort his friends had was that he had two gunshot wounds, so that he would probably be dead before the Zulus came to close quarters.*

The line about the comfort of his friends is a reference to the belief that the Zulus tortured and mutilated prisoners. In fact, although they did indeed 'desecrate' the dead – believing that the soul was released through disemboweling, and that a dead enemy's jawbone made an effective lucky charm – this probably did not extend to tormenting people who were still alive, however much those at the time (especially the horrified comrades who had to retrieve the distorted bodies) thought it did.

In his 'In Memoriam' notice in the school magazine Blaikie was described as 'a strong, roving, kind-hearted boy, not much in love with the discipline and regular work of a public school, but with an honest desire to do well' (it should be said, though, that a local history of Pietermaritzburg said he 'was long remembered for his remarkable intelligence'). The faintly freebooting style of the Natal Carbineers (Volunteers) and the 'independence and freedom of an open-air colonial life' must have suited him well; nonetheless, when he set out with his unit, 'contrary to his usual habit, he spoke very seriously of the risk he knew he was running.' Harry, Jim Blaikie's brother, identified him by a silver bracelet and his unusually large head. He would later be buried in his own grave, made of Scots granite, one of few casualties to have this peculiar privilege. His school in South Africa, now known as Maritzburg College, erected memorials to Blaikie and its other fallen old boys both on the battlefield and in its main building.

The *Fettesian* obituary's reference to Blaikie's widowed mother's hopes for her son, whose 'premature and awful death must have brought a peculiarly bitter sense of desolation' is one of the most stiffly touching elements in a generally robust publication. In his last letter home, Blaikie had asked his sister to tell his mother that he was reading his Bible. The importance of such messages to parents, in an age when youth was in perpetual danger of being cut short, cannot be overestimated. Victorian *Fettesians* carried just as many reports of untimely ends from illnesses and accidental injuries, which now might be treatable, as they did of old boys killed in battle; a diphtheria epidemic in 1883 carried off a pupil, Duncan Campbell, and required the boys to be evacuated to Windermere for a term until the school buildings could be decontaminated. The Headmaster's wife remained; she and her youngest son died. The school chapel's St. Cecilia Window commemorates the music-loving and loyal Mrs. Potts. There was soon a proposal that a memorial be erected to Blaikie. What is striking is that the rather prescient pupil making this suggestion in the *Fettesian* was perfectly well aware that Blaikie was most definitely not going to be the last to be killed:

Might we not erect a marble tablet in the College, on which to be engraved the names of Blaikie and those Fettesians whose fate it may be to die a soldier's death?... We hold up before the School the names of those who have won honours at the University. Surely those who die like Blaikie are worthy of a small space on our walls.

Plenty of opportunities were going to come the way of Fettesians to die like Blaikie; in December 1882 the *Fettesian* carried a comprehensive account of service in Egypt with the Gordon Highlanders, who were attempting to defeat Arabi Pasha's anti-European uprising and safeguard the Suez Canal. An anonymous old boy described the boredom, insufferable heat, confusion and occasional excitement of middle eastern warfare in a way that would surely be familiar to those who served there under Montgomery or those who would come later in Iraq and Kuwait. His accommodation, for instance, was 'fairly comfortable, except for mosquitoes, which were terrible: the place had been a good deal knocked about by the shells of the fleet, and there was one hole particularly noticeable in the wall of our sleeping-room, about nine feet across.'

The reach of modern technology, so crucial to British success, was also apparent in battle; when the 40-pounder gun battery opened up, the narrator couldn't really see the effect, except that lots of people were running about, 'so I fancy they must have been rather alarmed.' When he himself advanced (after 'a capital lunch') he and his men were grateful for the soft sand, which meant the enemy's shells buried themselves in the ground without harming anyone. It was a source of genuine pride to him that 'the kilts have never been anywhere but well to the front', though he did recognize their impracticality in the desert heat when 'one poor chap fell down dead on the spot from sun-stroke.' He gave a detailed account of the Battle of Tel-el-Kebir in September 1882:

It was four o'clock when an order was issued that parade was to take place at five, in 'fighting order', 70 rounds of ammunition carried, and water-bottles filled with tea... tents were to be struck at 6.15, packed and taken with such baggage as we possessed to the nearest point of the railway: the Brigade to fall in at 7 on the desert beyond the railway, and make a night march on Tel-el-Kebir: the enemy's position would be approached to within 200 yards, when the whole line would break into a cheer, the pipes commence playing, and the enemy's earthworks were to be taken at a rush...

What really impressed this unnamed warrior (probably Lt. R. S. Hunter-Blair, the only Old Fettesian in the Gordon Highlanders known to have served at Tel-el-Kebir, though not the only one at the battle as Capt. G. R. Cavaye also fought there with the Camerons) was that this plan was followed to the letter – and actually worked. Given that military cliché has it that elaborate planning never survives contact with the enemy, this was impressive. The British troops advanced across the desert in perfect silence, wondering if, in the pitch darkness, they had 'mistaken their way':

About a quarter to five, I noticed the ground seemed to be gradually rising as we advanced. A minute or two later three or four shots fired apparently about four hundred yards to our front in rapid succession, removed all doubts as to our whereabouts: without halting, the order was given to fix bayonets: they were hardly on, when a shell screaming high over our heads seemed to give the enemy the signal to open fire. A long line of parapet in front of us, not more than 150 yards from us, burst into a perfect blaze of fire, which was kept up steadily till we were into them.

The incessant roar of rifles, the thunder of artillery, the explosions of shells, the swish and ping of bullets over our heads, all combined to make the most fearful uproar imaginable, and of course hearing any word of command or bugle was out of the question. But none was needed, a deafening cheer, a thousand times more exciting than any words could ever have been, was raised along the whole line; one rush of seventy yards or so brought us to the trenches, and the ditch and slope to the parapet were gained. The enemy stood well so far, keeping up an incessant though wildly-directed fire; but as our men poured over the parapet, using the bayonet freely, it became more than they could stand, and a general stampede took place to the second line.

All this time no shot had been fired by us, and not until the second line of entrenchments was taken, was any shot fired at the now retreating enemy. It was at this time when those opposite us had been driven back that we suffered most. Very few had fallen while charging up the glacis; everything nearly went over our heads, but after the charge and when we were more or less mixed up with the men of other regiments inside the work, we observed a heavy fire being directed on us from a large redoubt some 400 yards to our left, which had not been captured. For about ten minutes this went on, and here and there men were being knocked over, while an endeavour was made to get them into some sort of formation.

Very soon this redoubt was taken, and a general advance was made through the position towards where the camp lay. There was no more opposition. The whole country before us seemed covered with men, hurrying off as hard as their legs would carry them: while our horse artillery, which had come into action splendidly some minutes before, poured shrapnel into them, and further away on the right, the Bengal Lancers were galloping up in pursuit.

Arabi Pasha surrendered, thus ending the war, shortly after this, and Hunter-Blair remarked that, although his current posting, Ghezrieh Camp near Cairo, was 'a most unpleasantly dusty spot', on the bright side 'there seems to be fair shooting to be got' and he concluded with the hope that 'an occupation of a few months ought to pass pleasantly enough.' Hunter-Blair, along with other Fettesians such as Captains M'Leod and Cavaye and Lieutenants Brack-Boyd-Wilson, Findlay and Sellar, was later to serve in the Nile Campaign of 1884-5 and in the Sudan in 1885-6; many were decorated for their efforts. At Fettes, the defeat in 1886 of the Islamic forces which killed the national hero General Gordon was hymned in such a way as to merge the optimistic vision of a peaceful, industrious Empire with a rather more bloodthirsty craving for revenge:

Thou standest where the rushing waters meet,
Thy white walls shining in the tropic sun,
And heavy lie thy shadows on the sand
That reaches out around thee; in the east
Are seen the distance skyward-towering heights.
Thou art at peace at last; the bloody wars
So often waged amidst thy dreary wastes
Are past for aye; thou shalt not see again
The tide of battle surge around thy gates;
The glitter of the sun strikes not today
The barbarous spear and roughly-shapen shield.
But in thy streets is heard the busy hum
Of those who barter up and down the world.
Yet 'midst of these scenes of peace, there lies a spot,
Beneath the palm-trees by the river's brink,
Which we do gaze on with a misty eye,
For there he died, a soldier undismayed;
Died like a hero – desolate – alone.
'Remember Gordon' do these rivers cry?
Yea, we remember; for the goal is won,
The vengeance is complete, for which we looked
So many years. And now hicks Pasha's host,
Metemmeh's raid with murder foul and black,
At last revenged. And though we were too late
To save our hero – only two short days –
The name of Gordon is not lost as yet;
The greatest Christian general of the age
Shall be remembered by all British hearts
With love and pride; and if he died alone,
Yet Death hath placed her laurels on his brow.
Khartoum and Gordon – Oh, thou cruel Soudan,
What misery thy hell-born hosts have given,
What shame have put upon the British Arms –
But vengeance is complete, so may his shade
At last find rest from struggle, toil, and war!

Short notes added to the school's Army List mentioned everyone who had seen combat, though none was to send such remarkably detailed news of his activities as Hunter-Blair had done. Charles Findlay, 'an athletic fellow, popular at the school' was later to die fighting the Dervishes at the Battle of Atbara in Kitchener's final conquest of the Sudan. A bestselling history of the campaign recorded his death:

...he had been married but a month or two before, and the widowed bride was not eighteen. He was a man of a singularly simple, sincere, and winning nature, and the whole force lamented his loss. Probably his great height – for he stood near 6 feet 6 inches – had attracted attack besides his daring: he was one of the first, some said the first, to get over the stockade, and had killed two of the enemy with his sword before he dropped.[47]

The *Fettesian* was pleased to record that Queen Victoria had taken a personal interest in Findlay's widow, giving her child – unborn at the time of Atbara – a baptismal gift and offering to stand as godmother. Another officer who fought at Atbara, 'frank, fearless and kind-hearted' Duncan 'Daddy' M'Leod, came to visit his old school after the campaign; 'he was as keen to talk over old times as he was reluctant to talk about himself or the events which led to his early promotion.'

Remembered with equal affection by schoolmates and soldiers for 'his kindly disposition, as much as for his pluck and manliness', M'Leod was to die, not in war, but in the notorious Thirsk railway crash of 1892. A signaller, distraught over the death of his child the previous day but forced to work despite his lack of sleep, accidentally routed the London to Edinburgh express into the path of a goods train, killing M'Leod and nine others. A subsequent court case established the contributory negligence of the railway company, which was presumably of little comfort to the relatives of the casualties but did at least establish a precedent for the future. A poem about M'Leod was quoted in the *Fettesian* Christmas number in 1892:

He braved the battle's roar;
He stood the foe before;
He nobly fault and bled.
In sultry eastern climes
Death passed him many times,
Yet never touched his head.

At soldier good and true!
Whene'er the bugle blew,
MacLeod was at his post.

Pluck was his guiding star,
He'd fain have died in war,
Facing a hostile host.

It was not thus to be;
This was not Fate's decree;
Fate willed another death.
A train speeds through the gloom;
A dash! - a crash! - his doom!
He's drawn his latest breath.

Written by 'H.E.G.', (not an Old Fettesian, it seems) this originally appeared in the *Weekly Scotsman*, an indication of how popular M'Leod was in Scottish society. By a tragic coincidence, another OF, Lt. Eric Salvesen, was one of over 200 Royal Scots killed in the Gretna train disaster of 22 May 1915.

The Battle of Tel-el-Kebir, from a contemporary report

8. Restless Natives

Fettesians sent their alma mater tales of life, both military and civilian, elsewhere in Africa; Alexander Miller Graham wrote from Mashonaland in 1890 describing the progress of the British expedition there, which was intended to overawe the locals in the name of the Queen and add to her dominions. He was full of excitement at their progress through the 'splendid high country', and how rumours that an impi of Lobengula, King of the Matabele, was abroad led to the formation of a laager of well-armed wagons.

A subsequent letter on the 'Matabele Difficulty' in 1893, however, had a more harsh tone; he explained that the British South Africa Company had been forced to take action against some of Lobengula's men after they 'actually had the audacity to pursue Mashonas into Fort Victoria, killing some of them in the main street. Of course this was too much for the whites, and they promptly turned out and shot some thirty of the marauders.' Lobengula was, unsurprisingly, incensed at this, and Graham's letter concluded that peace in the region would depend on driving the irritable monarch across the Zambezi; 'many good men will be killed before that is accomplished.' Lobengula was defeated, partly through the use of Maxim guns, in the First Matabele War.

An 'account of an Old Fettesian's adventures', taken from a South African newspaper, appeared in the *Fettesian* in March 1894. It described how Graham, 'a hearty and well-connected Edinburgh lad', was seeing a lot of the 'adventurous side of South African life.' After service in the Pioneer Corps in Mashonaland, he was put in charge of the Labour and Transport Department of the British South Africa Company. The bulk of the report, however, was taken up with an account of a hunting expedition:

> *They spent three weeks at Zumbo, shooting plenty of hippos, and having some good days with the buffalo in the fly; but it was on their return journey that their greatest luck befell them. They came across six white rhinos. Eyre shot a mother, while Coryndon and Graham shot a babe. Next morning they also caught another little one alive. They tried very hard to keep it in life with a view of bringing a £500 curio into Salisbury. They had no milk, however, and the interesting animal would*

not take the grass they tried to feed with. Although they tried to lead it on their journey back to Mashonaland, and did their best for it, they only kept it alive for seven days. The mother was stuffed and sent to the Chicago Exhibition, where she created a big sensation.

Mr. Graham also shot an enormous lioness one night at eight feet distance with a Martini-Henry bullet, whilst under his trading wagon. He carries one of the big teeth on his watch-chain as a trophy. Mr. Graham is a man we shall hear more of.

Sadly, this was all too true. Graham, who became the Native Commissioner at Inyati in Matabeleland, was one of a group of whites besieged and subsequently massacred in the native uprising of 1896. The *Scotsman* said that he had 'met a soldier's death' with his colleagues; 'they might probably have saved themselves by seeking refuge in Bulawayo, but they no doubt scorned to desert the district which was placed in their charge.' He was not the only Old Fettesian caught up in the rebellion: George Lennock was also killed, his body 'almost unrecognisable' when found, and Jim Normand was one of the settlers who helped suppress the natives. This uprising was partly encouraged by tales among the tribesmen of a mystical, messianic leader, and was the inspiration for Buchan's *Prester John*.

Norman Alexander Wilson, another colonial officer and 'a great favourite with all who knew him at home or abroad', was to die in a mutiny by Sudanese mercenary soldiers in Uganda the following year. The Sudanese had initially rebelled out of discontent about pay, but seem to have developed ideas of creating an Islamic state. Along with a Major Thruston, Wilson was 'treacherously' seized by supposedly loyal troops and imprisoned in Lubwa's Fort.

After a fierce firefight with the remaining Europeans and Sikhs, some of the mutineers were on the brink of surrender, but the officers, Bilal, Mabruk and Rehan, decided to stiffen their resolve by executing the British prisoners. Thruston apparently said contemptuously, 'If you are going to shoot me, do so at once, but I warn you that many of my countrymen will come up, and that you will have cause to regret it.' He and Wilson were promptly shot, as was another British soldier called Scott who had attempted to escape. This ensured that there would be no turning back by soldiers who were having second thoughts about their rebellion, which was eventually crushed by a British expedition, one of whose officers was another Old Fettesian,

Capt. W.M. Southey of the 27th Bombay Infantry. Wilson was buried with the others in the churchyard of the Church Missionary Society on Namirembe Hill in Kampala.[48]

In West Africa, several Old Fettesians ran similar risks as the Empire's bounds went wider yet. In 1900, 24 British officers and 700 locally-recruited troops entered Northern Nigeria, warned by Sultan Attahiru that he would 'never agree with you... Between us and you there are no dealings, except as between Moslems and Unbelievers – War.' The British imposed client rulers and, faced with a charge by thousands of Africans, machine-gunned them to traditional effect. They then held a grand ceremony at which the populace was assured that their customs and religion would be respected so long as they obeyed the laws of Queen Victoria. Old Fettesian Featherston Cargill, who had been in Africa since 1895 and taken part in a variety of expeditions attempting to impose the imperial order, became the British Resident at Kano.

Unfortunately, British actions had simply inflamed religious and patriotic feeling, and with Attihiru still at large Cargill wrote to his superiors in a panic warning of a jihad. Matters became worse when another local leader announced that he was the new Mahdi, leading a holy war against the infidels. A small British force suffered an embarrassing reverse at Burmi before their superior firepower finally crushed the revolt; the decapitated heads of the defeated leaders were photographed for the edification of other would-be opponents of the spread of civilisation. Radical Islam, and of course resentment at the British occupation, remained a problem for administrators for decades.

Cargill attempted to reorganise Kano, replacing assorted Islamic forms of taxation with a uniform poll tax and imposing a system whereby an Emir was the sole native authority and his chiefs were regional representatives. He attempted to bring Sharia law into line with British legal norms and to dissuade the local nobility to dismantle their elaborate institutions of slavery. He took the progressive step of befriending a number of ex-slaves. Although he was awarded the CMG in 1905, his incessant reforms irritated both his bosses in London and the local aristocracy, as well as introducing unwanted instability into the lives of the peasantry with his attempts at economic innovation. He retired to Britain as early as 1909, and is not widely regarded by historians as a success – a recent study of early British colonial policy in Northern Nigeria was bluntly titled *Cargill's Mistakes*.

The British Army was becoming more expert in fighting Africans and its losses in battle, especially with the introduction of the machine-gun, were comparatively small. African resistance and rebellion, bloody and terrifying for civilians caught up in it though it was, ultimately failed within a year or so, crushed with the swift ferocity the Army had learned through the centuries. For Fettes, the casualties seem to have reached double figures just before the beginning of the Boer War, and the suggestion that a memorial be set up was finally acted upon. The 'Memorial Brass' was announced in the *Fettesian* in November 1898. It was to be erected in the school chapel to honour those 'killed while in the Imperial Service' – Blaikie of Isandlwana, Findlay of Atbara, MacLean of the North-West Frontier, Graham of Matabeleland, and Wilson of Uganda – though not the dozen or more victims of accident or disease ('The decision as to whether a name is to be inscribed or not, to be vested in the Headmaster, without appeal'). Subscriptions of up to ten shillings were invited, the cost being estimated at £30. C.J.N. Fleming, Old Fettesian and Scottish rugby international, was treasurer of the appeal. Other names would be added – sooner, and in greater numbers, than anticipated, for the Boer War was about to break out.

Imperial troops attempting to rescue the unfortunate Norman Wilson and other Britons seized by mutineers (from H.H. Austin, With MacDonald in Uganda, *1903)*

9. The Boer War

Not all Fettesians went out into the world with formal training behind them, good business connections, or military service to look forward to; many really did head off into the Empire in the hope of making a fortune from scratch. For this sort of adventurer South Africa was, quite literally, a gold-mine. An anonymous OF wrote to the school in 1896 to describe how he had turned up in Johannesburg to 'try my luck.' He was taken on by J. Hubert Davies, an electrical engineering firm servicing the mines, as a workman on £4 per week, with the promise of promotion after a month if he proved he was 'worth anything'. £4, he wrote, was quite low in comparison with the £7 earned by foremen and skilled technicians, but he could easily live on it, spending about £10 in a month on his living expenses and trying to save as much as possible. On pay-day, the first Saturday of the month, every man in the place went 'into town on the spree' and thought nothing of spending £10 in an evening; other surplus cash was spent in stock exchange dabbling. He had some useful advice for his successors:

There is no doubt that this is a splendid place for any fellow who has had a mechanical training, and is prepared to start low down and work hard. It certainly is hard work, but I think one is certain to get on by sticking to it... There are an enormous number who come here with a gentleman's education and expect to drop at once into a good job. But they soon find their mistake. I must own that I had thoughts of finding a better job than I have present, but I soon found that it was necessary to start the bottom, and am now not at all sorry for it.

Lurking behind this vision of streets paved with gold were simmering tensions which would erupt into the Boer War. In contrast with the wars against black Africans, generally less well-equipped than the British, the South African or Boer War was not settled quickly. Defeating them was a huge enterprise; the school magazine published specific lists of old boys serving there, running to around 80 names in total, a remarkable number for a school which had only reached a population of 200 in 1890. Tensions with the Dutch-speaking Boers or Afrikaners had been building for some time; there had been a brief and, for Britain, embarrassing war in 1880-1. In 1888, 'J.G.B.S.' wrote to the school to report that the King of Swaziland cracked open the champagne 'after ascertaining we were not Dutch' and that in the mining town of Barberton there had been 'a very fair prospect of an anti-Dutch riot'.

Serious fighting finally broke out in 1899, but both British and Boers had been spoiling for a fight for several years in squabbles over mineral rights, the independence of the Afrikaner Republics and the grievances of English-speaking 'Uitlanders' in Dutch-speaking territory. There were several provocative incidents, most notoriously the raid by the Matabeleland Administrator Dr. Jameson in 1895-6, in which two old Fettesians, 'Pat' Normand and Sydney Bowden, participated. Normand, who had been prevented by a knee injury from joining the British Army, had gone to South Africa in the hope of becoming a gold-miner, and walked 300 miles from Mafeking to Bulawayo, where his brother Jim worked. Joining the Matabele Mounted Police, he was recruited by the British South Africa Chartered Company as a Corporal in 'C' Company for the raid, but was captured along with his comrades. Unable to pay the fines required by the Boers for their release, Normand and Bowden were deported back to Britain.[49] Ironically, it was probably the denuding of the area of troops by the raid that permitted the Matabele uprising which killed Lennock and Graham (whom Jameson had personally appointed) to spread out of control.

After several years of agitation, the affronted Boers issued an ultimatum for British forces to back off in the autumn of 1899. This was greeted with hoots of derision in the British press, as the army, which had seen the trouble brewing, already had thousands of troops and much modern equipment either in or en route to South Africa in readiness to crush these strange Old Testament figures. Fettesians were there from the outset, and within a few months of the outbreak of war the school was receiving the doleful news that several had already been killed.

The British officers who sailed south in 1899 were supremely confident in the reforms and experience of the army. As one of the most recent histories of the war argues, 'if ever a war looked as if it was going to be over by Christmas, it was this one.'[50] The senior military commentator Henry Spenser Wilkinson proudly announced that 'the Army was never in better condition either as regards the zeal and skill of its officers from the highest to the lowest, the training and discipline of the men, or the organisation of all the branches of the service.'

The British also genuinely believed that they were in the right, and that this was a war of principle for fair governance in South Africa, something which only they could bring. This message had been trumpeted in the loyal dominions of Canada, Australia and New Zealand, and they supplied volunteers to add to those flocking to the colours at home. Fettes' expatriate volunteers included Robert Cowen of the Australian Bushmen, whilst doctors George Buchanan and John Cowan offered their services; local settlers like Vincent Corbett and Sydney Bowden also joined up. The British were armed with modern weapons, including early machine-guns, and had developed sophisticated supply techniques.

Unfortunately for them, the Boers had been busy making preparations too, stocking up with modern weapons of their own including French artillery and German rifles. They made use of their knowledge of the countryside and avoided taking part in too many pitched battles, where the superior British numbers would count against them. General Kitchener expressed the general disapproval felt by the high command for the new enemy's tactics in a letter, complaining that 'the Boers are not like the Sudanese who stood up to a fair fight. They are always running away on their little ponies.' The Boers were presumably aware that the Sudanese at Omdurman had been massacred by machine-guns and were not inclined to share this experience of 'fair fight.'

Although less disciplined than the British, the Boers showed great initiative in exploiting their enemy's weaknesses, and were aided by foreign volunteers from Holland, Germany, France, Ireland, America and Russia, most of whom had professional military experience – in the case of the Irish, often with the British Army. This was not going to be over by Christmas.

A letter to his father from Pat Normand, serving with the Imperial Light Horse – a force which had been organised in a mere three weeks, so thick on the ground were suitable troopers in the southern Africa of the day – gave some indication of how difficult the war was going to be. He made light of his wound received at Elandslaagte in October 1899, and dismissed the heavy casualty list from the battle by saying that 'although it appears heavy, still we taught the Boers a good lesson, and showed them that British soldiers could face any hail of bullets.' His concluding thought was that 'if there is a big engagement, I expect it will finish the war... the soldiers are all in excellent spirits, and I am sure they will give the Boers a good licking.' As the rest of his letter shows, he must have been aware that this could be interpreted as rather optimistic, given the facts, which as he admitted were that a quarter of his unit were dead or wounded, that the Boers had fought to the end, having to be bayoneted by the Gordons and Manchesters (regiments he was too modest to admit that his colonial rough-riders rescued from defeat) and that, in the meantime, the British had been forced to evacuate the mining town of Dundee.

At the same battle, another Old Fettesian, Capt. Matthew Meiklejohn, 'received three bullets through his upper right arm, one through his right forearm, one through the left thigh, two through his helmet, a wound in the neck, one of his fingers blown away, and his sword and his scabbard were shot to pieces.' A few months later, the *Fettesian* began with an article headed 'Our First Victoria Cross':

Just as we are going to press we learn from the London Gazette *that the Queen has been pleased to confer the decoration of the Victoria Cross for conspicuous bravery in South Africa on Captain Matthew Fontaine Murray Meiklejohn, Gordon Highlanders. Captain Meiklejohn was recommended for rallying the men after losing their leaders and wavering, and leading them against the enemy's position, where he fell desperately wounded in four places, at the battle of Elandslaagte last October. Subsequently he had his right arm amputated. We may well be proud of Captain Meiklejohn, who has been the first Old Fettesian to gain the Victoria Cross, and we hope he will be but the first of many who will gain this distinction, and whose names will ever be held in high honour at Fettes.*

Despite the casualties, that month's rhyming editorial was optimistic:

The war in the Transvaal is nearing its close,
Where Roberts and Powell have settled our foes,
So there's almost no news to report from the front,
Where the A.M.B. bravely is bearing the brunt,
Save that several O.F.s have been winning a name
By rising a step on the ladder of fame.

The 1900 'Vive-la' shared this optimism, reflecting the (premature) hopes of imminent victory which followed the relief of Mafeking:

In Mafeking's honour we scored a whole holiday,
And shared their relief from hard work by a jolly day:
And we quite hoped another would come for Pretoria,
But only shared there in the Honor et Gloria.

With our cheers let us all make the old Gym. resound
For O.F.s who are fighting on Krueger-Steyn ground;
And now that things there are beginning to shake down,
May they help the New Company 'Kart'Oom to Cape Town.'

It is worth noting that sporting heroes occupied a much larger section of the 'Vive-la' than military victory – David Bedell-Sivright, who was to be one of the greatest Scottish sportsmen of the age, was mentioned three times for his 'footer' exploits for Fettes, Scotland and his university.

Elandslaagte had been a hard victory for the British, and it was followed by several humiliations known as 'Black Week' in December 1899. First, General Gatacre was defeated at Stormberg, partly through his over-ambitious idea of repeating the Tel-el-Kebir night march over much more complex and hilly terrain. Then Lord Methuen attempted to march to Kimberley, taking the entrenched Boer positions on Magersfontein Kop with the same method, adding the more traditional elements of an artillery bombardment followed by a Highlander charge.

Unfortunately, the Boers were not on the Kop, but at the bottom of it in trenches, and the shelling only wounded three of them, so the dawn probing by the Highlanders was met with furious resistance which inflicted heavy casualties and forced the British to retreat. The British suffered almost a thousand casualties, the Boers less than a third of that, and the leading units of the Highland Brigade lost 60 per cent of their officers.

Fettes' losses included J. Rutherford-Clark of the Seaforth Highlanders, an experienced officer who had been with the regiment since 1882, and W.B. King of the Argyll and Sutherland Highlanders, who had not seen active service before. Douglas Monypenny of the Seaforths survived Magersfontein only to die as a result of wounds received at Paardeberg in February the following year. He had been a keen sportsman, 'one of the finest all-round athletes ever produced by the School', winning the prized Challenge Clock for running, captaining various teams and, just after leaving the school in 1898, playing rugby for Scotland. The *Fettesian* editorial, after rejoicing in British successes, turned to the 'view of the War which cannot be lost sight of – the solemn side'. Listing the casualties, it commented:

We feel Monypenny's loss most as, having left us most recently, and we are sure that we are only expressing the feelings of all who knew him, in saying that he was one of the very best, loyal to his school and his country.
The advent of the frost has proved a great nuisance, and has wrought havoc with the fixture card...

The magazine subsequently carried a poem, 'To D.B.M.':

And art thou sped, light-hearted comrade, thou
Our schoolboy hero one brief year ago?
Thy country craved thy strength, and thou didst go
To fight her battle, should thine hour allow.
Already hadst thou seen stern fights enow:
We marveled at thy prowess, thews, and speed;
Thou wast not as thy fellows, and the meed
Of larger worth seemed destined for thy brow.
Thou hast not failed us: in the roll of fame
Among the elect there is nor first nor last;
Who nobly does, does best in small or great:
And when the final call to duty came,
And thy young life was on the waters cast,
Well didst thou strive, we know, and take thy fate.

Slightly more cheerful news came with the Relief of Ladysmith, during which Normand was again wounded whilst standing up to point out enemy positions to his Commanding Officer. He was to win the DSO twice (the second was cancelled on the grounds that it could only be won once) and receive three mentions in despatches. His home country would honour him by making him a Burgess and Freeman of the Burgh of Dysart. At Fettes, when the news about Ladysmith came through, the Headmaster granted a half-holiday and the boys made merry; the money for medals at the school sports went to sponsor a Fettes bed in a front-line hospital. Young patriots bombarded the school magazine with poetry so jingoistic even the *Daily Mail* might have been alarmed. Several sub-Kipling efforts appeared, such as this one, entitled 'Tommy on the War':

We have lately called on Steyn
In his home in Bloemfontein:
But he'd gone, vamoosed, with all his wrongs to Reitz;
For he'd bolted like a bullet,
With a biltong in his gullet,
And his heart a-flopping down among his lights.
No, he hadn't time to stay,
And pass the time of day,
And show us round his bloomin' city sights.

Oddly, this was written by a former master, H.F. Morland Simpson, who had gone from Fettes to become Rector of Aberdeen Grammar School. He also wrote one about the naval guns which had been dragged overland to relieve Ladysmith:

Oh, he ain't no Jack-a-dandy,
But he's hearty, smart and handy,
When you've run among the rocks and jammed her tight;
Then it's "Bless your tarry phiz,
Can you help us out o'this?"
Sweetheart's kisses ain't so welcome, by a sight.

So he came up at the double,
Just in time to share our trouble,
And he brought his brace o'beauties, trim and long,
On the wheels that Scott invented,
With the shell's that's yaller-scented,
"Lady Ann" and "Bloody Mary" goin' strong.

And it warn't no picnic, too,
For Lambton and his crew;
Ladysmith was pressin' and they'd got to stay.
Gordons, Manchesters, and Devons,
How they loved those four-point-sevens,
And the tars who helped 'em keep the Boers at bay!

Morland Simpson was a highly respected intellectual, an expert on primary education, antiquities and runes, and the most charitable assumption to make is that he was overcome by patriotic fervour, or perhaps keen to show some sort of solidarity with his former pupils, especially those killed. His poems appeared just after a letter from an actual soldier who described life on board one of the troopships – where there were seven

Fettesians, all from the same house, Glencorse – in tones so measured as to render the experience rather boring. It mostly revolved around the meticulous arrangements for looking after the horses.

This was followed, 25 pages later, a brief announcement to the effect that David Rew had been killed in action. Further information came through later from one of the other Fettesians in his unit, the 23rd Imperial Yeomanry; the Boers had attacked them at dawn, and when Rew's Colt machine-gun jammed he was killed trying to fix it. Another Fettesian in this engagement, C.B.C. Storey, 'was splattered all over the face with bits of lead... how his sight has been spared to him is nothing short of a miracle.' The British got their heavier weapons working and the Boers 'funked it and fled, leaving seventeen dead' – something of a Pyrrhic victory since 'I was appalled to find that we had lost twenty-five killed and four wounded.'

There were later reports of two more Imperial Yeomanry Old Fettesians dead in South Africa: George Frederick Shaw ('a promising football player') and 'Ben' Grieg, remembered as 'singularly massive and powerful'. G.L. Greene of the Madras Survey Department, it was announced, had also died of cholera in India. In November 1900 the *Fettesian* editorialized, with cautious flippancy:

...it is extremely gratifying to find that Fettes has not been behindhand in doing her best for the Empire. Not only is the School well represented in the regular army, but when the call came, many O.F.s volunteered. This enthusiasm extends to present Fettesians as well; for when some 'gentlemen in khaki' dined in hall before starting for the front, the cheering and singing were enthusiastic and inspiriting. These gentlemen showed themselves true not only to their country, but to the traditions of the School as well – by asking for a half-holiday... Our masters, too, are keen patriots. Some, however, are not so keen on the War, for they find that the Army Class and accordingly their work have increased alarmingly.

As the last deaths were reported to the school, it was noted with pride that Lt. William Thomson of the Royal Munster Fusiliers, a keen cricketer, had been mentioned in Lord Kitchener's final despatches.

In December 1900, the school magazine announced that work was to commence on the memorial, and named those who were to appear on it. By this stage, Lt. Douglas Oliver of 2

Battalion, Norfolk Regiment, had died at Myistroom on 27 August 1900, of wounds received in action two days previously.

Four months later came the news that another old boy was dead; Bernard Armstrong Hebeler, killed at Hartebeestfontein on 18 February 1901. He had sailed to South Africa at his own expense, and had been 'conspicuous for his gallant behaviour', carrying a wounded comrade to safety under fire and carrying on fighting, despite a leg wound, until he was shot through the head. His Captain wrote that 'there was no better or braver soldier in the whole regiment' and a fellow-trooper added that he 'met his death, where he always was, right in the very front.' A small plaque was put up as a memorial in the school, but as it did not have a name on it, someone put it in storage during refurbishment and it has only just been rediscovered.

The plaque at Fettes in memory of Bernard Hebeler

Hebeler's would be the final name on the memorial, but it can reasonably be argued that at least several others ought to be on it (had there been room on it, which there is not). G.G. Smith, of the Natal Volunteer Ambulance Corps, was killed at Spion Kop trying to bring water to the wounded, 'struck by a shell and literally smashed to pieces.' Oddly, despite a letter to the school saying that his commanding officer believed he deserved the VC, he does not appear on the war memorial in the chapel. Nor does George Coulson, who 'died of malarial fever contracted in service in South Africa' nor Claude Auldjo Jamieson, whose his horse, shot by the Boers, fell on him; badly injured, he returned to Scotland to die in September 1902.

Neil James MacVean, a teacher and field sports enthusiast, had joined the Imperial Yeomanry and died on Christmas Day 1902 in Pretoria of enteric fever, probably the same illness that carried off another OF, George Shaw, whilst William Smith died of typhoid at Kimberley at around the same time: the war had fanned epidemics among the troops – not to mention amongst Boer civilians in the concentration camps. The memorial also fails to mention others who were dying elsewhere in the Empire. Just after the Boer War, Bengal Lancers John Nairne Durrant Steuart and John Lindesay Stewart died of enteric fever in various parts of India, as did the gallant Lt. William Thomson. Of the fallen in the Matabele Rebellion, Graham is on the memorial but Lennock is not. Recent research by Fettes historians suggests that no less than 21 OFs died on service before the First World War, but have no memorial as yet; another dozen died between the wars.

After the war ended, accident continued to carry off Fettesians in South Africa and elsewhere; Alfred Valentine Pulford was struck by lightning at Pietermaritzburg in January 1904, and on Christmas Day 1907, Capt. Hugh Stanton Craig drowned, with his wife Nell, in a boating accident near Maraisburg. Capt. George Rothney Lamb of the Royal Garrison Artillery, a veteran of the Miranzai Expedition of 1891, was killed by a fall from his horse on Salisbury Plain when the beast was startled during a live-firing exercise. A local farmer saw the horse charging down a hill, out of control; Lamb was found unconscious and bleeding, and died later.

It may be that, since that illness could carry off boys in the school itself – Guy Hamilton Ziegler, aged sixteen, and John Kerr Anderson, aged eighteen, died within a week of each other in 1898 – it may not have 'counted' as anything other than an occupational hazard of life itself. That is not to say that the school was blasé about it. In 1887 Fettes had been quick to expel a boy from the West Indies who was believed to have leprosy; when he sued for breach of contract, the judge, whilst accepting that leprosy might not be contagious, found in the school's favour, noting that the existence of such a disease in the midst of a community of boys 'was calculated to create such terror as to impair the usefulness of the institution.'[51]

A poem appeared in 1900 which summed up the views of the school, and much of wider society, about the losses.

At Britain's call to these, her gallant sons,
To fight for fatherland, what joy they felt!
They little thought that they would be the ones
To be struck down in battle on the veldt.

Yes so it was; right royally they tried
To help in furthering proud Britannia's rule;
They went where Duty pointed – and they died,
And swelled the roll of honour of their School.

When time for parting came, they were prepared,
And cheerfully they bade their last farewell
To those who hoped and prayed they might be spared,
Who loved them and who mourned them when they fell.

They shall not be forgotten; side by side
With us short years ago they lived and moved:
Remember those Fettesians who have died,
And thus brought honour to the School they loved.

Although it is not apparent from the *Fettesians* of the period – schoolboys not being, as a rule, privy to the discussions of a closed circle of politicians and generals – the military world was about to change again. As Barnett puts it:

The Boer War had shattered the Victorian complacency of the
British ruling classes, if not of British public opinion. It had
demonstrated the feebleness of the land forces of the British
Empire before a gloating world: it revealed how alone Britain
stood in that gloating world... after 1900, Britain's relative
power was sharply diminished right across the globe.[52]

At the time, this was not understood, and Fettes was confidently to continue to supply the human material for all aspects of the Empire for decades to come. Four of the forty-five non-English officials of the Sudan Political Service were O.F.s (though an astonishing 15 had attended the Edinburgh Academy).[53] The sporting accomplishments and sound schooling which the Victorians saw as central to the future imperialist's training gave the Sudan its nickname: 'the land where blacks were ruled by blues.'

Their confidence can be seen in the work of Henry William Auden, a Fettes master who became Principal of the prestigious Upper Canada College in Ontario in 1902. Faced with the threats of American influence and vague stirrings of separate identity, Auden promoted Empire Loyalism and the superiority of Britishness to young Canadians through publications such as *Simple Rules of Health and Courtesy for Those at School* (1911) and, of course, sport. He wanted more immigration into the colonies, announcing after a trip round the Canadian west that American settlers, who knew the soil, might be most ideally suited if they could be persuaded to stay. His other favoured groups were Scandinavians, the Doukhobors (a Russian pacifist sect), Galicians (Ukrainians, Poles and Jews from Eastern Europe), and Englishmen – who he found a little disappointing. Best of all, of course, was the 'Scotchman.'[54]

Memorials in the school chapel to the Old Fettsians killed fighting for the Empire, and to those who never left school but died whilst still pupils.

10. Haldane's Army

The Anglo-Boer War, as it now tends to be called, has a number of extraordinary resonances for today's observer. It split opinion violently; in favour were the political right, including Tory government ministers and MPs, plus the rowdiest newspapers such as the *Daily Mail*, and the jingoistic parts of all social classes. Their aggressive nationalism was rather too much even for that ardent imperialist Rudyard Kipling, who disapproved of civilians 'killing Kruger with your mouth'. The left, that is, part of the Liberal Party and the socialist movement, was less gung-ho, and was assailed as 'pro-Boer' by jingoists, although in fact they were also keen to see Britain win so long as victory was cleanly won and magnanimously imposed.

One such was one of the first Old Fettesians to become a Member of Parliament, John Deans Hope, who was elected to Westminster in 1900 to represent West Fife. Hope's membership of various radical committees is what has identified him to historians as a 'pro-Boer' – he made no speeches and asked only nine questions in the House in almost a quarter of a century, so cannot be said to have made a great impact for the cause. Irish nationalists, by contrast, openly rejoiced at England's failures and many went to fight for the Boers.

Britain's European neighbours, who had so slavishly paid obeisance at Queen Victoria's Diamond Jubilee in 1897 – *Le Figaro* going so far as to say that Britain had surpassed Rome – were gleefully hostile, and, as previously noted, supplied the Boers with weapons and volunteers. In distant Haiti, where Vernon Hesketh Prichard was exploring at the time of the war, the Francophone press summoned up the spirit of one of Britain's old foes:

Napoleon, risen from his tomb at the Invalides, addresses his old soldiers: The English, the eternal enemy who conquered you — for in conquering me she conquered you — the English of Trafalgar and of Waterloo, recoil before the energy of a little people of Africa... Albion fights no longer... Albion dies...

Admittedly, the Haitians were not desperately familiar with the exact circumstances of the war; one of their (many) generals hoped the Boers would win because 'Boers were negroes persecuted by the British.' Major Barnes, serving in China with the international forces fighting the Boxer rebellion, was irritated by a German's views on the subject:

> *As we had halted at the same time we got into conversation with one of the officers, who spoke perfect English, and in due time asked him if there was any news. His answer was startling:*
>> *'Yes; the Boers have retaken Pretoria.'*
>> *This struck me as being a somewhat needless falsehood...*

Anger at the critics, both domestic and international, was occasionally apparent in the pages of the *Fettesian*. There was a sense that any criticism of the war and 'our boys' was tantamount to national betrayal – one certainly gets it from the later verses of Morland Simpson's poem, where he gloatingly described the dispatch to St. Helena of Boer generals and foreign volunteers in their army, and then turned his ire on Britain's critics:

Now his old familiar Cronje
Is away with Schiel to "Boney"
And with him gone a lot of foreign scum,
To a rocky pocket isle,
Just eleven hundred mile,
Where the nearest port on earth is Kingdom come:
Hochaddled Meinheer Prussians,
And die-for-freedom Russians,
German Grafs – war correspondents when they're caught –
French Counts, United Staters,
Blake's blackguards, Fenian traitors,
And the Red Cross Ambulancer sneaks who fought.

There are still at home, I fear,
Some we'd gladly have out here,
If they'd only put their flippers up and fight:
Shrieking Schreiner, and resetters
Of the Clerk who boned those letters,
And the sweeps that's always shoutin', "Serves you right!"
The peace-at-any-price
Labby, "Jawson", Stead, and Bryce,
Who will prove you – for a dollar – Kruger's white.

Those sympathetic to the troops lambasted the government for not supplying them well enough. Will Ogilvie was a friend of the flamboyant Australian horseman 'Breaker' Morant, executed for killing prisoners in the Boer War, and defended him as a cavalier who should have been in the service of King Charles, 'full of romance and void of fears.' Nonetheless, as the war progressed with pointless British losses and evidence of atrocities against civilians, more criticisms emerged at home, of which the soldiers in the field were undoubtedly aware. The Boers' tenacity in fighting and their real suffering in the concentration camps were widely covered by the world's press. Even members of the government had their doubts, Arthur Balfour noting to the cabinet that were he a Boer he would be reluctant to accept what the British had to offer. The widespread view that it was not a war of principle or for civilisation, but for what lay under the earth, and thus being fought on behalf of greedy capitalists, further undermined the cause.

Another issue was the alleged faults of the British Army itself. The sheer scale of the numbers involved, of course, made it all the more likely that the public would take notice; whereas 30,000 men had gone to the Crimea and 16,000 to Egypt, 448,000 troops went to South Africa in a campaign which cost £230 million and almost 22,000 British and imperial dead. On only two occasions since the Crimean War – at Isandlwana and the lesser-known battle of Maiwand in Afghanistan, neither of which was really typical – had British Army lost over a hundred men in a single engagement. This was happening all too frequently in South Africa, and an irritated officer wrote that the British 'did not know that bloodshed was a usual consequence of the armed collision of combatants. This led to the hysteria with which they received the news of casualties.'

Journalists stirred the pot further, also much to the fury of the professionals. Leo Amery's *Times History of the War in South Africa*, published in a succession of enormous volumes between 1900 and 1909, claimed that the Army was 'nothing more or less than a gigantic Dotheboys Hall.'

Although harsh, judgments like these were both common and widely believed, and led to public demands for further reform. These were often mixed with the faintly sinister eugenic notions of the period, especially the issue that the great British race might be in decline in its industrial cities. Darwinism, some feared, might go into reverse and humans might stumble backwards. Victorians and Edwardians loved the idea of progress and could not allow this decline to happen. Hence the creation of bodies like the Inter-departmental Committee on Physical Deterioration in 1903, special attention being paid to Glasgow, where some of the most shockingly underfed and enfeebled recruits had emerged.

The health of the nation's youth was given special attention, and it can even be argued that improved conditions in public primary schools were less the gifts of compassion than the products of an elite fearful of national weakness. Like all schools, Fettes paid attention to the need to keep an eye on physical development. In March 1900 Charlie Fleming, the games master, published a detailed five-page report on the six-year study he had been making of the boys' measurements; this included graphs and copious statistics. The former Scotland centre had, with his assistants, conducted up to 20,000 measurements to establish that the average Fettes sixth-former weighed 10 stone 2.15lb and was 5 feet 8.26 inches tall with a 36.5 inch inflated chest and a 13.55 inch calf. Fleming did not comment on this, or indeed present any significant analysis other than that the graphs showed boys grew quickly, but the average British adult male of this period was around 5 feet 6.5 inches tall, noticeably shorter than the Fettes lads.

Charles Fleming

By the time the South African war finally ended in the middle of 1902, the Fettesians were no longer Victorians. They marked the old lady's passing with the cancellation of both lessons and games and an 'interminably long and depressing' memorial service in chapel. Lockhart remembered that he 'wandered aimlessly about the corridors and prep room munching biscuits and afraid to raise my voice, not so much from respect for the dead monarch as from fear lest a prefect would reprove me for making a noise.'[55] He doubted the wisdom of enforcing the solemnity of death on small boys, who tended to be bored by it, and where their emotions were affected 'the reaction is generally mawkish and unhealthy.'

John Spencer Muirhead believed that although little had changed outwardly in the school, with the 'ancient rigour' of Victorian tradition visible to all, 'new ideas were in the air' at Fettes. Games, classics, and a sensible approach to religion (none of the 'precious religiosity which saps the moral vigour of many schools' but 'utmost delicacy' of respect for each man's faith) were still in place; teaching modern languages was still a 'thankless task'; and music suffered from an organ with 'severe indigestion' and a lack of good voices. Nonetheless, 'un-Victorian' tendencies were appearing. The background music to these came in the form of 'Alexander's Ragtime Band', one of the most popular pre-1914 hits 'wafted over the Atlantic', and a new form of technology:

In the studies preposterous claims were bandied for the virtues of preposterous motor-cars, and fags gained brief notoriety for the accuracy with which they could reproduce from the pit of the stomach the sounds of gear-changing in horizontal-cylindered Wolseleys, whose entrails were surprisingly draped round bonnets shaped like the fronts of whales.

John ('Ian Hay') Beith encouraged discussion which 'seemed a fair substitute for the somewhat over-emphatic Kipling'. Such progressive thought extended even to 'the rights of the Lower Orders' and 'advanced opinion deprecated the traditional ferocity of one House to fags as being beyond an enlightened treatment of the servile class.' Politics could be 'a vague subject of disquiet' if there was the risk that one's friends' sisters would 'follow one's aunts in their unseemly courses'; on the whole, though, the changes at Fettes were welcomed.

The military world, too, was about to change again. As Corelli Barnett put it, the Boer War shattered the Victorian complacency of the British ruling class because 'it had demonstrated the feebleness of the land forces of the British Empire before a gloating world'. Cardwell had not been enough, it seemed.

The war in South Africa which should not have taken (so far as the optimists were concerned) more than a few months had dragged on for three years. Moreover, to some extent it had been won by the 'methods of barbarism' which split British society – the use of concentration camps, Kitchener's scorched-earth policy, and the ill-treatment of civilians. The British defeats had shocked a public, which, whilst used to the occasional noble martyr of the Gordon type to eulogise, did not expect such regular and major setbacks.

A Royal Commission into the war, published in 1903, criticised the army from top to bottom and in every branch. Transport, supply, planning, training and manpower – both quality and quantity – all were at fault. The private soldier was all too often unfit and ill-educated: this came as no news to the army, which knew perfectly well that in its present state it was not something a fit and educated manual worker would choose to join. This led to a lack of resourcefulness on the battlefield, but the training too was at fault, for the iron discipline of the old close-order tactics which worked well in the eighteenth century, when other Europeans used it, and also against undrilled tribesmen, was of little use against guerrilla warriors like the Boers. If anything, it just gave them easier targets.

Nor were the officers above criticism. Despite Cardwell, there were still many 'from a leisured class to whom professionalism too often appeared as vulgar careerism.' Knowledge and skill were less important than money and style in the most prestigious regiments; the Akers-Douglas Committee investigating officer training was told that 'keenness is out of fashion... it is not the correct form.' Barnett notes that 'in the cavalry, where living expenses were highest, professional standards were said by the Report to be lowest.'

It was found in South Africa that the army was aided enormously by the experience of local settlers (like Fettes' unlucky Blaikie and the more successful Normands) who knew the countryside and had acquired fieldcraft skills both from the natives they fought and those they recruited, and who formed 'rough-riding' volunteer units in the Imperial Yeomanry – 'accustomed to horses and wide open spaces, enterprising and intelligent' – they were infinitely better than the allegedly pampered darlings of the regular cavalry regiments. Interestingly, Fettesians seem to have been unwilling or unable to spare the cash to join the latter, but they were heavily represented in the former. There were by 1900 at least half a dozen former Fettes pupils serving in various colonial mounted units, and twice as many again in the British volunteer yeomanry. It was the infantry, however, which those who joined the Army most often entered. (This is not to say that there were no Fettesians of gentle birth – there was a sprinkling of titles, and an even larger number of impressive pedigrees, in the army lists.)

Fettesians were also, as we have seen, found in considerable numbers in India. The Indian Army was in some ways the antithesis of the British, because its British-born officers were mostly recruited (like William Fettes' in-laws) from the upper- and middle-middle class. Professional soldiering was a job to them. They were, accordingly, slightly looked down upon by the fancier regiments of the British Army. This did not stop them from surrounding themselves with an aura of aristocratic splendour whenever possible. Old Fettesian Capt. A.I.R. Glasfurd published *Rifle and Romance in the Indian Jungle* in 1905. This enthusiastic hymn of love to the joys of big-game hunting was a thrilling read for the pupils, and must have inspired at least some to emulate the Captain's adventures:

> *In the distance a glow of little fires shows some of our men occupied with their evening meal, and a murmur of voices behind the camp discloses others, who are engaged in rubbing wood-ashes into a certain broad peg-stretched skin. Yes! It has been a lucky day, and the first tiger is already bagged. Happy thought that prompted the placing of an extra 'stop' at the very spot which he should choose to break out of the beat, and a fatal pause that which he made, right under our tree! A shy, game-killing beast of the denser jungles, what long, weary ways his tracks had led us that hot day, until we 'ringed' him, at home, so far from his 'kill' of the previous night! And so he is slain over again. Anticipation, realisation, fond recollection; threefold charm of these forest scenes; pleasures that will be ours long after the jungle knows us no more!*
>
> *The white sheets look invitingly cool in the moonlight; and the cheroot can be finished there. 'Call me at five o'clock, Abdul!' How delicious to stretch one's pleasantly fatigued limbs on the smooth linen, and gaze up at the thought-bringing stars, while dreams of the morrow's sport trail gentle sleep in their train. So the East doth call to us who are her foster-children.*[56]

Captain Glasfurd goes tiger-hunting: an illustration from one of his books

Captain Glasfurd would have met plenty of his school contemporaries when not pursuing India's wildlife. In 1907, the *Fettesian* printed another Army List. It showed 56 OFs on active service with the Indian Army – 14 in the cavalry, 34 in the infantry and four medics. All, of course, were officers. A further 114 were (or had been when they died) in the British Army, and 47 of these had been decorated, mostly for service in South Africa. Of these, 20 were in the cavalry, and only three of these were regular officers in prestigious regular regiments – Maj. J.W. Ferguson, 20th Hussars, Lt. G. Macleod, 16th (The Queen's) Lancers and Lt. W. Duguid-M'Combie, 2nd Dragoons (Royal Scots Greys) who contributed to a regimental history in the 1920s and lived until 1970, when he was 96, and had outlived most of his contemporaries, their regiments, and the Empire they served. The band of the Scots Greys marched up the drive his estate at Easter Skene, Aberdeenshire, to mark his ninetieth birthday.

The other horsemen were mostly non-commissioned or, in a few cases like that of P.L.A. Gabbett, held honorary rank; the vast majority were members of the Imperial Yeomanry, though H.E.C. Anderson served five years in the ranks of the 20th Hussars, retiring in 1905. He rejoined the Army and became an officer in the 9th Leicesters when the First World War broke out. By contrast, all 54 of the Old Fettesians serving with infantry regiments were officers, over half of whom were in Scottish regiments.

There were also 25 OFs in various artillery regiments, eight engineers, five doctors and two in the Army Service Corps, and there were three Royal Marines. 15 were in the Reserves, 12 in the Militia, 20 in the Volunteers (most of whom did not hold commissions) and 11 were retired – a grand total of 241. Of the regulars, 61 had seen active service in South Africa, 22 on or near the North-West Frontier, ten in various parts of East Africa, and others in Burma, China, Tibet, and Aden.

The service records of some of the career soldiers were remarkable. Major E.W.M. Norie of the Middlesex Regiment, first commissioned in 1883, served in Burma in 1887-9 and on the Chin-Lushai expedition of 1889-90, was a signaller with the Malakand Field Force in 1897 (the punitive expedition on the North-West Frontier immortalised by Winston Churchill), worked extensively in military intelligence, took part in, and wrote the report on, the crushing of the Boxer Rebellion in China, was an adviser to the Egyptian Army, and became Aide-de-Camp to George V. In the process, as previously noted, he had lost an arm to a dum-dum bullet. His brothers also had stirring careers; Charles served on the North-West Frontier (where he too lost an arm), in the Boer War and on the Salonica Campaign of 1916, whilst Frank was assistant commander of the Apa Tanang expedition to the North-East Frontier and won the DSO in France in the Great War, later becoming a spiritual healer.[57]

One more unusual record at Fettes is for Kenneth D. Robinson, who was appended to the military list as having fought in Theodore Roosevelt's 'Rough Riders' in the Spanish-American War in Cuba. Such an exotic connection will have been impressive enough for the boys, but those who read Roosevelt's own account of the war would have been delighted to learn that he caught the eye of the future president:

> *Kenneth Robinson, a gallant young trooper, though himself severely (I supposed at the time mortally) wounded, was noteworthy for the way in which he tended those among the wounded who were even more helpless, and the cheery courage with which he kept up their spirits.*[58]

Robinson, a wealthy real estate agent who lived on Broadway, was one of several wealthy New Yorkers to join in the ranks, young men of substance and style who 'grasped the opportunity to join Roosevelt's regiment and desert the ballroom for the malarial fields of Cuba.' 28 Fettesians were recorded as having died in service, 17 through disease or accident, nine in combat and two in native uprisings; seven had been severely wounded, losing limbs and eyes.

A contemporary illustration of a British field hospital in Africa

The army's increasing concern to recruit the best possible officers led, by the early twentieth century, to the establishment of the commissions for graduates scheme, whereby a young man could simultaneously study for a degree and undertake basic training through a university's volunteer company and its military lecturer. Capt. Johnstone, formerly of the Royal Engineers, was Edinburgh University's military lecturer, and he wrote several times to the school in order to advertise the scheme through the *Fettesian*, the last appearing in December 1913, less than a year before war broke out. Pressure groups such as the Navy League also tried to drum up support for stepping up expenditure on capital ships, and bombarded the *Fettesian* (and any other publications aimed at the nation's youth) with letters on the topic of maritime supremacy. As Fettes made its way through the Edwardian era, there was a sense of nervous excitement for any strategically-minded lad who paid attention to the newspapers.

11. Top Nation

It is often argued that the sense of national superiority Europeans possessed in the late nineteenth and early twentieth centuries contributed to the climate of war in 1914. Hamilton Fyfe, writing in old age after having witnessed as a journalist revolution in Mexico, the First World War, and the outbreak of hostilities in 1939, argued that:

From the time when the Hebrews were told by their fanatical, and therefore slightly demented, leader Moses that they were a 'chosen race' appointed to wipe out other races and seize their territory, the idea that nations have characters and missions has frequently tormented and devastated the world.[59]

This was not the view of his contemporaries. With cheery self-assurance forming the background to their global dominance, some of the opinions which the correspondents to the *Fettesian* express about those they encountered abroad are undoubtedly a little jarring to modern ears: 'a despicable race they are, lazy, cruel, but withal good-tempered enough as far as grinning at you goes when you chaff them... in habits and sanitation they are simply filthy,' to quote, for instance, George Dillon, writing about the Burmese. People at that time spoke of foreigners in a way which would not be normal now.

However, whilst the British, in the words of Old Fettesian W.C. Sellar in *1066 and All That*, saw themselves as 'top nation' before the First World War, but plenty of them could see qualities to respect in others. Many young imperialists were appreciative of the other peoples among whom they worked, as Walter Cook's 1895 letter to the *Fettesian* from Afghanistan shows:

...let us have a glance at them as they swing along beside us. They are chiefly Sikhs and Pathans. The Sikhs, tall, straight, strong men with well-cut regular features... they have little superfluous flesh and plenty of hard muscle... their moustachios curled and brushed upwards give a fierce expression to their faces, while their tout ensemble *is eminently soldier-like.*

*The Pathans show rather larger bone than the Sikhs, and
are perhaps on the whole bigger men. Many of them have fair
hair and blue eyes, which go well with their high and somewhat
Scottish features; in fact they remind one not a little of our own
highlanders at home. Inured to all kinds of hardship among
their wild and almost inaccessible mountains and well
accustomed to face danger in the prosecution of their numerous
blood-feuds, they enlist in our ranks, savages it may be, but
with little to learn as light infantry soldiers.*

Dillon, too, admired the Sikhs: 'no English troops with full
accoutrements carrying rifle and forty rounds of ammunition
could have marched 82 miles in three days in intense heat as my
Sikhs and I did.' He was also deeply impressed with the way his
men refused to take cover whilst he himself was in the open.
Major Arthur Barnes, in his account of his service with the now-
forgotten Chinese Regiment (raised in the British leased territory
of Wei-Hai-Wei and used to suppress the Boxer rebellion) hoped
to give a positive picture of the 'loyal' Chinese at a time when
they were being generally stereotyped as treacherous and cruel.
'No one who has served on the same side as Chinese, as we did,
will ever allow it to be said, as it is so often by the ignorant, that
they are cowards.'[60] He pointed out that in the capture of
Tientsin the Chinese Regiment was the only British unit to enter
the city with the predominantly Japanese assault.

Vernon Hesketh-Prichard, exploring Haiti ('first of the
Negro republics') was impressed with the country people's
honesty and generosity – 'never once would my hosts, however
poor they might be, allow me to pay for my entertainment.'[61] 'I
have accepted the hospitality of his roof and lived with him,'
wrote the explorer of the black peasant, 'and, apart from his
natural laziness and his inclination towards snake-worship, have
found him a simple and unobtrusive being.'[62]

Hesketh-Prichard concluded his detailed examination of
Haiti by addressing directly the idea which lay at the heart of
British (and French, Portuguese, and Belgian) justification for
governing large swathes of Africa: that 'the Black man... cannot
rule himself.'[63] What was a young Fettesian of that era to think
when he read this, as so many undoubtedly did? So far as they
were concerned, this was no bar-room racialist bigot but an
intelligent and courageous observer (not to mention a highly
successful professional cricketer who scored over 7,500 runs for
Hampshire and the MCC, so presumably a trustworthy sort of
chap) who had thoroughly explored a black nation, recognized

the qualities of its people, and reached what he believed was a balanced conclusion. The British, in their imperial pride, had either forgotten what their ancestors had been like, or assumed that the United Kingdom's apparently rapid ascent from primitive squalor to industrial wealth was due to some sort of superior quality which other people lacked.

Hesketh Vernon Hesketh-Prichard, from Hunting Camps in Wood & Wilderness *(1910)*

Present-day schoolchildren are astonished and horrified by this sort of thing, but not so long ago, it was not only common currency, but believed to be common sense. It is worth saying that Hesketh-Prichard was perfectly well aware of the inadequacies of his own people, writing in another of his books that:

The attitude of the young Britisher abroad towards the rest of the world in general is at once a source of great national strength and of serious national weakness. First, as we know, he is a poor linguist, who prefers to go on speaking his own language, and, when not understood, attempting to enforce comprehension by the very simple expedient of shouting louder... By his attitude in this matter — an attitude dictated partly by a too common lack of the linguistic faculty and partly by a certain rooted conviction that a man who cannot speak English is a man of 'lesser breed' — the Britisher has to a certain extent forced English upon a very unwilling world.[64]

His readers felt it was the duty of the British to steer their black brothers towards the path of righteousness. As one historian of Empire, R.H. Heussler, put it:

The Briton was an underpaid schoolmaster in an over-populated school. He lived in the house and took a full part in its life, without ever crossing the line. He knew the boys well and liked them and sympathized with their problems. His discipline was unyielding and fair, and it was as constant as sun and rain.[65]

The Old Fettesian in colonial service saw himself much as he would have seen his housemasters; a mixture of teacher and policeman, as well as judge, priest and all-round fixer, helping the people of his district just as the boys of his house had once been helped towards adulthood by its tutors. Two letters from old boys, both serving the Empire, were received in 1895 which explicitly mentioned this as their ideal. John Anderson wrote in the 1920s that:

The quality of the civilisation of the North American continent, which has been my dwelling-place for more than twenty years, has many features which are a patent improvement upon the parallel standards of Europe, but it is only now beginning to acquire schools like Fettes where the lesson is taught that the claims and interests of the individual should be as dust in the balance beside the obligations to a common society. When such schools have been multiplied a hundredfold in North America, there will be cleaner politics, better business morality, and a better brand of patriotism.

Various military historians have commented on how the army was both less jingoistic and less racialist than the Victorian public; as George Orwell pointed out, the attitudes ascribed by Kipling to imperial troops were not as hypocritical as those back home (Barnett blames the distance between the British and the Indians on 'stern memsahibs, stiffly corsetted with Victorian morality and etiquette and resentful of the voluptuous competition of sari-ed brown bodies' – a notion with which at least one OF, as we have seen, would have agreed). The British tried to be less genocidal and cruel than either the Germans or Belgians, and sometimes intervened to stop bad behaviour towards 'natives' – most famously by abandoning slavery and then forcing everyone else to do so. Major Barnes, stationed in China with the international forces, was disgusted at the behaviour of other Europeans in the looting which followed the Boxers' defeat:

I have seen officers, of foreign troops, be it well understood, wrangling with soldiers of their own and of other armies over articles that possibly neither wanted. No doubt foreigners say this sort of thing went on in our force; but I am proud to think that such could never have been the case, for our discipline was, on all points, far away above that of our Allies as a whole.

Serious incidents emerged when Japanese soldiers began abusing the populace, the Germans shot an old man at random, and the locals begged Barnes for protection because they were afraid to harvest their crops because they were afraid of the Russians. Barnes wrote that, 'It was a very liberal education – as indeed was the whole campaign – on the ways of various nationalities who may not always be on our side.'

By the time he died in the late thirties, Barnes would indeed have seen his country fight the Germans, Austro-Hungarians and Russians, and be on its way to fighting the Italians and Japanese, all of whom had been his allies in China. Of the international forces in China in 1900, only the Americans had not fought Britain at some point, which would not have surprised Barnes: 'The Americans were, as was the case all through this queer war, our great friends, and for all that politicians may say and papers write, I am convinced that the campaign has done more than fifty old treaties to bring the two nations together.'

Of course, he saw the British as the natural leaders of humanity, inspiring those who fought for them against their own races with such confidence that the gospel of British benevolence was spread by word of mouth. On one occasion, the international forces had to borrow some junks to sail up-river to relieve Peking, and the Chinese Regiment proved ideal ambassadors for this task:

Our men, after a little, inspired the villagers and others with great confidence, so much so that large numbers naturally preferred to take service willingly with us and be certain of pay, rations, and good treatment (points on all of which our men were well able to reassure them), to continuing their present riparian existence with no certainty of any of these good things, and the constant risk of visits, the reverse of friendly, from other less well-disposed 'foreign devils.' Naturally, all our crews were not entirely volunteers, some requiring a little more or less gentle persuasion to get them to join our glad throng, and to remain once they had come, but the majority were quite glad of the chance.

Arthur Barnes as a newly-commissioned lieutenant in the Wiltshire Regiment in 1886, when he was around 19 years old; he served in India and Burma as well as China, and took part in the retreat from Mons in 1914.
(Picture supplied by Mr. Fred Larimore)

The average British child generally had little contact with foreigners at that time, unless he lived by a port, but Fettesians were taught by several. School mythology abounds with tales of the Czech art master, Mr. A.F. Bohuslav-Kroupa, who 'exerted not the slightest control over his classes' which accordingly degenerated into a 'bear-garden'; in the school's centenary book of reminiscences, John Spencer Muirhead recalled shamefacedly that 'it is chastening to contemplate what torments generations of Fettesians inflicted on a charming old gentleman.'

Ineffectual he may have been as a schoolmaster, but 'B-K' had a remarkably exciting pedigree; his valete in the *Fettesian* said there was 'certainly no master, probably few men in the kingdom, who had led a life of more stirring adventure: always in every crisis taking the weaker side, always defeated, and keeping to the last the unbroken, high-souled, chivalrous spirit.' He had studied art in Paris, lived as an Indian in America, explored the line for the Canadian Pacific Railway, invested in a mine which would have made him a fortune had it not caught fire, then made his way across Central America, where he was robbed by brigands. Thrillingly, he had worked in a bar (which he 'had to vacate suddenly as an irate American, for whom he had mixed the wrong cocktail, was looking for him with a shooting-iron'), sold fruit and drove a mule which powered a public cistern, before catching 'Yellow-Jack' fever and having to treat himself on a quarantine ship in Havana harbour.

His military experience began in the war between Russia and Poland, which was struggling to regain its independence: 'with this war Mr. Kroupa had no natural or special concern, but it was a war between a strong side and a weak one, and to a nature as chivalrous as his that was enough – he must go and help the weaker side.' He also fought as an Austrian officer against Prussia at Sadowa, and was lucky to escape with his life; the boys believed that his oddly-shaped head was the result of having been had been scalped by an enemy sabre.

Kroupa's departure was marked by an 'all-nighter' by the common room; apparently the retiree was the last man standing, still singing into the dawn. To this day, old hands tell new teachers and pupils alike about the memorable school report he produced about one of his charges: 'He is a horrid little boy. I hate him.' Kroupa's successor, the diminutive Welshman Morris Meredith Williams, was warned before taking up his post at Fettes that he must stamp his authority on the boys.

It is not known how well 'B-K' got on with 'Froggy' Goldschmidt, the Head of Modern Languages, of 'Prussian birth and Hebrew origin', who had been called up to fight in the Franco-Prussian War whilst teaching at Loretto. He must have found Fettes, with its (relatively) intellectual and international outlook, something of a relief. Almond, Loretto's headmaster, loathed foreigners, telling his wife that 'there is scarcely a sanely living man in the lot, so far as I can hear from those who have been abroad' (which he never had) and, when challenged by a language teacher on a point of honour, retorted 'you take me for a German.'

Prussian methods were clearly more effective than Bohemian ones – Goldschmidt would hurl the property of 'careless or stupid' Fettesians out the window. 'Many a time have boys passing beneath, and even masters, seen such a shower come hurtling through the air, to be recovered by a rueful youth expelled from the room with abusive banter.'

Regardless of their school experience or acquired imperialist views, former pupils who had dealings with foreign troops often spoke of them with respect. The Russo-Japanese War of 1904 was noted in the school magazine because of several Fettes connections and because of its impressive modernity. Lt.-Col. William Grant Macpherson, one of the most prominent 'patriarchs' and a distinguished officer in the Royal Army Medical Corps, was attached to the Japanese forces in Manchuria and was awarded the Order of the Sacred Treasure for his work there; he would later be a British Delegate Plenipotentiary at the Geneva Convention of 1906, write the official history of the RAMC in the Great War, and end his career as that corps' colonel commandant.

Lt. James MacNair Smith, who had represented the Royal Marine Light Infantry at the old queen's funeral, was serving with a squadron in the Pacific and visited Port Arthur, which the Japanese – then Britain's glorious allies for their part in humiliating the loathed Russians – had taken from the Tsar. He found the Japanese 'most polite and friendly', and on seeing the extent of their military achievement, commented that when their soldiers saluted the British officers, 'it ought to have been us who took our hats off to them.'

The battlefield at Port Arthur offered an insight into what was to come – Smith wrote that the fortified hillside had cost 10,000 Japanese and 5,000 Russian casualties, and the Japanese Navy had fired 20,000 tons of metal at it, whilst trenches, saps, tunnels and counter-mines, not to mention savage hand-to-hand fighting for every inch of ground, had characterised the fighting. The idea of the Japanese as Britain's allies must have seemed bitterly ironic to the Old Fettesians who fought in that most cruel of wars in the Far East in 1941-5.

The Japanese were not the only future enemies to get a good press at Fettes. The Germans were regarded reasonably affectionately, at least until they expressed sympathy towards the Boers in 1899-1902. One of the Patriarchs wrote that during the Franco-Prussian conflict of 1870-1, raging just as Fettes opened, 'we were keen partisans, and it is odd to recall that about five were "German" to one "French" – I suppose from a wish to be on the winning side.' In 1882 it was the French who inspired one of the many 'war scares', when a plethora of thrillers depicted Britain's closest neighbours as invading via the channel tunnel, then widely believed to be on the point of construction, disguised as tourists and waiters.

At that point, the Germans were, by contrast, harmless, engagingly different but not unpleasantly exotic like certain other nations. W.B. Adam, whose engaging memoirs of life at Fettes in 1914 and in the wartime Royal Navy are one of the delights of the school archive, recalled one of the servants overhearing two Germans deep in conversation, and commenting 'Ain't it wonderful how them two fellahs can understand each other, talkin' like that?'

There were occasional German pupils at Fettes, such as Edward Süwerkrop from Düsseldorf, who became a distinguished scientist and engineer in the United States. Eugen Florian Emil von Keudell and D.G. Schulze would later find it prudent to change their names to Murray and Miller. Schulze had been born in Glasgow and played rugby for Scotland, but clearly felt in 1919 the need formally to announce that he would henceforth be known by his mother's maiden name.

A number of enthusiastic Fettesian musicians attended the Deutsche Sängerbund Fest at Hamburg in the summer of 1882, and wrote very affectionately of it. They were undoubtedly impressed by the 'quiet, sober Germans' in the Bourse, the excellence of the arrangements for the song festival, the incredible quality of the music, and the fact that 'people were there to listen – not to be seen or talk'. A further trip to the Wagner Festival in Bayreuth in 1889 also gained a glowing review:

It is impossible to give anything like a true description of what is indescribable even to oneself. One is completely carried away; one's own personality and all the petty egoism of the outside world is utterly forgotten. It is like a new kind of life, where music is the medium by which the emotions are expressed, a medium far more subtle and expressive than mere words.

The Germans would doubtless have been impressed with this boundless enthusiasm – here was at least one Briton who understood the romantic intellectual soul! Cecil Reddie positively idolized the Germans and wrote copiously about how British schools (and everything else) could benefit from their ideas, emphasizing practical learning and cooperation rather than abstract classics and pointless competition:

> *Germany is, undoubtedly, the best organised, and most progressive country in the world at the present time... England will yet have to learn many lessons from Germany, if our Educational System, our National Organisation, our Philosophy and our Religion, not to speak of our Army (and, we fear too, our Navy) are not to remain very largely the wonder and astonishment of the world for antiquated absurdity. Their willingness to learn from abroad is the secret of their success, as our British ignorance and prejudice are the cause of our backwardness and will be the probable cause of the Decay and Dissolution of our Anglo-Keltic World-Dominion.*

In 1906, H.W. Auden, the former sixth form master at Fettes who had gone to Canada, observed in his book on the study of Greek that 'where Germany leads educationally, we may usually follow with advantage.' The *Fettesian* was even proud to report in 1908 that Kaiser Wilhelm II had conferred the Order of the Red Eagle (Second Class) on former pupil Lt.-Col. R.S.F. Henderson, a distinguished rugby player (Blackheath and five English international caps) and military medic who would later serve in the First World War.

A less respectful view came from an OF who wrote from Marburg University in 1890 that the German student, whilst as hard-working as his British equivalent, 'may be best described as a beer-drinking and fighting animal.' He gave a faintly bemused account of the duelling which undergraduates 'see as their most important sport.' Members of two clubs would slope off to a rural pub and then, clad in leather aprons and 'iron spectacles', proceed to 'rain in blows at each other's head and face, the only objects of attack, with what seems to the spectator terrible violence.' The correspondent regarded this as 'a form of vanity which we cannot understand' and concluded that that football was undoubtedly preferable.

What is now called a 'duvet', was seen at that time as a bizarre Teutonic eccentricity, and an awful 1902 poem entitled 'Made in Germanye' refers to the 'bulbous bagge' under which no true Briton could be expected to get a decent night's sleep. A German appeared as the comedy villain, Count Donnerwetter-Ueberunterhinterberg, played by Mr. Rhoades (later a supply organiser on the Western Front) in the masters' theatricals of Christmas 1910. The review of this performance – 'we should have liked to hear him repeat his magnificent name a little more frequently' – was written by R.H. Gordon, later to distinguish himself as a skilled wartime pilot.

By this point, attitudes were definitely changing. Hamilton Fyfe looked back on the situation thirty years later, and blamed a jingoistic press and government policy:

Up to 1904 most of the English had regarded the French with suspicion, with self-righteous disdain, as immoral, flighty, frivolous. France had been their enemy throughout the centuries; and as for its morals, well, look at Paris! The English had also up to that date considered Germans almost as honest, as serious, as home-loving as themselves. This was what they were taught.

Suddenly they were told to reverse their opinions. The French, they learned, were a noble folk, sadly misunderstood. Look how fond King Edward was of the Parisians, and they of him! As for the Germans, they were trying to steal Britain's trade; they aimed at building a navy to rival the British; they were a danger, must be very carefully watched. If they wanted war...[66]

As late as July 1914, though, there were friendly encounters with the future enemies of civilisation. William Neve Monteith, an OF of 1890s vintage, was sailing on the SS *Manila* off Norway when he was invited on board a German battleship:

We were shown over the ship, we were treated with the utmost courtesy and consideration, we were shown how the big guns were handled and the idea of pointing them at British ships was treated as a jest: 'It's what they were made for, no doubt,' was in effect what the Germans said, 'but they will never be used for that.'[67]

Monteith was later killed at Loos. The most negative view of the Germans written by an Old Fettesian in this period came from Major Arthur Barnes' account, written in 1901-2, of the international effort to crush the Boxer Uprising. He was deeply unimpressed by an attempt by the Germans and Russians to capture the Pietsang forts without waiting for British help, a 'miserable fiasco' which cost the arrogant continentals dozens of casualties (the Italians, who refused to advance without the British, were spared – the 'one bright feature' of the affair). Although, to be fair, the relative ease of communication made

114

slights from them more obvious than those from the Japanese, who arguably behaved with the greatest brutality, Barnes was more disapproving of the Germans than any of the other nations:

> *...we found all the officers of that nation who passed through — and they were not a few — always very friendly. As far as I can ascertain, however, there was something in the air of Peking and its environs that made them somewhat arrogant and not very friendly either to us or to the Americans. Perhaps... they imagined that they were the only pebbles on the beach, and acted in accordance with that idea. This seems to have been the case, more especially in the later days, when, possibly, they had learned all they could from us, and thought they could then afford to be rude.*

Barnes also quoted with obvious approval a newspaper report which compared the relative utility of the British and German approaches to warfare and the leadership of foreign troops:

> *The difference between the English and German soldier is not spiritual, but national... The individuality, capacity for initiative and independence of the Englishman have made him supreme in the world; the German, who readily submits to authority, and lacks self-reliance, has been forced to play a lesser part... how is it that Germans so signally fail to rule foreign peoples?... That our system of education is defective may be admitted; that the sense of duty is more highly developed in Germans than in ourselves must be denied. By their works ye shall know them.*

Even the most dedicated patriot might have been aware that the Germans signally failed to rule foreign peoples not because of any failures on their part but because the British and French had largely beaten them to it. This report, incidentally, came from *The Broad Arrow: A Paper for the Services*, which was published by the government and presumably reflected at least some of the opinions of the British high command. The First World War would soon demonstrate conclusively that the German soldier had, in fact, many dangerous qualities.

12. More Armed Rehearsals

Barnes' efforts did not go unnoticed back home. The poetic editorial in the Fettesian in July 1900 contained the lines:

But though in the Transvaal the war's nearly done,
In China we feel sure it has only begun;
Still, several O.F.s have already gone out,
And we hope they will soon put the Boxers to rout.

The Boxer Rising, as it is generally known, was a violent protest against the foreign financial institutions and Christian missions which had been penetrating the Empire for decades. Seizing Peking, and declaring the Dowager Empress their figurehead leader, they besieged the legation quarter and launched attacks on foreigners and local Christians throughout North China. The British, Americans, Russians and Japanese, with support from France, Germany, Italy and Austria-Hungary, retook Peking with great slaughter and looting.

Fettesians were represented here just as they had been in South Africa and on the North-West Frontier. The official account of the punitive campaign was written by one of them, Frontier veteran E.W.M. Norie, but that by his younger colleague Arthur Barnes (who, as we have seen, led a locally-recruited regiment from the British enclave at Wei-Hai-Wei) is much more entertaining.

Barnes was breezily indifferent to why he was fighting – 'Who or what was responsible I do not consider it within my province to inquire, or even to conjecture' – but was proud to note that one of his comrades had struck 'the first blow of a long series which China has since been dealt, to show her that the Western barbarian has come to stay.' Barnes's brutal candour should be set against his genuine feelings of horror at the 'appalling' atrocities committed by the Boxers.

Corpses there were, naturally, in large numbers, most of them in fairly advanced states of decomposition, and covered with flies. In one place we came upon an entire family, from all appearances, huddled together and almost hidden by a perfect canopy of flies. Most of them, children of tender years, had received wounds of a nature such as to put all hopes of recovery out of the question, even had the victim been a strong man, and out of which the mother, herself badly hit, was striving, in vain, to keep the swarms of noxious flies. It was a sad and gruesome sight, but there were worse, the mention even of which can serve no useful end.

He did, incidentally, admit that this particular area 'had been exposed to our fire on the one hand, and the depredations of the Boxers on the other', so it is not impossible that these were the victims of British artillery – the account is not entirely clear, but it seems more likely that he was referring to the results of enemy action. Whatever the case, it is as unromantic a depiction of the horrors of war as one could wish for. He was impressed by the power of artillery – which was to be the biggest killer on the Western Front a few years later – noting on one occasion when a British shell hit a Chinese magazine:

The explosion that followed was one of the most lovely, and, at the same time, the most extraordinary, sights I have ever seen. A huge pillar of snowy whiteness rose slowly and majestically into the air, and when its summit was five or six hundred feet above the earth, it slowly opened out like a vast sunshade, and after hanging in the air for ten minutes or so, slowly dissolved. I have since seen summer clouds of similar appearance, but never anything to surpass this death-dealing cloud for the beauty of its pure whiteness.

Like Old Fettesians a century later in Afghanistan and Iraq, after the fighting Barnes found himself responsible for law and order in part of the conquered territory; although not specifically trained for the task, the British officer was supposed to use his common sense and ideals of fair play and act as mayor and policeman when the previous holders of these posts had fled:

I found a good deal of employment in the early part of the day, owing to the large number of merchants, mostly outside the wall, who came or sent to complain of looters. I went out with a party on several occasions, and was the means of inflicting summary punishment on a lot of palpable scoundrels who seemed to be not behaving nicely. All these merchants wanted British protection, and as this seemed to be a free issue, consisting merely of a notice to that effect in English and

French, and as the petitioners were, to all appearance, quite peaceful and law-abiding, most of them got their wish.

Barnes saw the defeat of the Boxers in global terms:

Without doubt the teeming millions of China were watching, with eager eyes, for the outcome of this rude arbitrament of war, either to rise in their strength and expel the 'foreign devil' once and for all, or to lie low, perhaps, for another opportunity. Nor must we forget the anxiety of Europe, either merely commercially, or for the safety of friends, not only in Peking and Tientsin, but all over China. The issue was, of a truth, far more momentous than can be gauged by the blood that was shed to bring it about.

People who witnessed such a victory for the power of Western, and especially British, arms over such a vast country could hardly be expected to believe that the nation's power was waning.

Another imperial struggle which attracted the school's attention took place in what is now Libya, though on this occasion there were no former pupils fighting. Just before the outbreak of the Great War, the *Fettesian* was pleased to note that another OF, William McClure, had written a highly-praised account of Italy's war in North Africa. McClure's book is a fascinating insight into the thinking of military-minded imperialists in the years immediately preceding the Great War.

Italy had angered most of her neighbours by seizing what is now Libya from the crumbling Ottoman Empire, and, like the British in South Africa, attracted international condemnation. McClure, an early 'embedded' journalist with the Italian forces, robustly scorned the rest of the world's 'hypocrisy and forgetfulness.'[68] Believing that the Italians must play a part in the civilising mission of all white men, he defended the use of force as necessary when dealing with less developed peoples – 'in order to win an Arab by words it seems essential to demonstrate that behind the will to persuade lies the power to compel.' McClure painted a savage picture of the 'Mussulman' way of war whilst brushing aside any talk by 'atrocitymongers' of excesses by the Italians. Coming upon a 'ghastly scene' at El Hanni, where the mutilated bodies of fifty tortured Bersaglieri had been dumped, the Italian soldiers impressed McClure with their 'controlled and dignified behaviour.' Any reprisals taken by the Italians were 'fully justified' and 'errors and excesses, however regrettable and blamable, were not unnatural or altogether unpardonable.' Arab violence, by contrast, consisted of 'unprintable obscenities', 'hideous scenes of cruelty and mutilation, outrages committed upon the dead and wounded while the battle was still raging.'

Like the British, McClure believed, the Italians were bringing the advantages of modern medicine to the dark continent, and he paid tribute to their doctors' efforts in stamping out cholera and malaria. The methods might have been severe – 'the streets were liberally sprayed with disinfectants, with the result that the manifold odours of Turkish Tripoli were soon submerged in the all-conquering smell of carbolic' – but so far as he was concerned this was a small price to pay for the advantages of civilisation.

An even more exciting glimpse of modernity came from above, for this was the first war in which air power was heavily and successfully deployed. Fettes had played its own small part in the development of aviation: former pupils Frank and Harold Barnwell of Stirling made Scotland's first powered flight in July 1909, a brief hundred-yard hop at a height of fifteen feet. The Italian airships and aeroplanes left McClure 'firmly convinced of the practical value of aviation.'

An Italian airship; an illustration from W. McClure's Italy in North Africa

Although he was most thrilled by flights of 140 miles, then a great feat, he believed that reconnaissance and mapping were the most likely uses of aviation. Bombing, the war's key innovation, 'does not appear to have been attended with any great measure of success, and it is not unlikely that the possibilities of early development in this direction have been exaggerated.'

The school magazine proudly reprinted the glowing reviews McClure's book received in the *Spectator* ('probably the truest estimate of the work and conduct of the Italian Army in Libya that has been published in English') and the *Westminster Gazette* ('undoubtedly the most level-headed and critical account of the Italo-Turkish War'). These appeared on the same pages of the November 1913 issue which reported over a dozen military, political, imperial and educational promotions achieved by former pupils, including the news that Lewis Robertson was now captain of London Scottish – the pinnacle of achievement for many Scots living in England. Did the keen militarists at Fettes take on board the lessons of this war? We cannot be sure, because the school's copy of *Italy in North Africa* was erroneously placed in the travel section of the library, where it remained for several decades.

13. A Passionate Appeal to our Patriotism

Fettes tried to do its best to keep boys informed about the great events of the world around them. Speakers with magic lantern slide-projectors, such as Captain Reade, who spoke to the boys about the joys of the Royal Navy in November 1895, were regular and popular additions to the curriculum. A month later, Professor Prothero spoke on Imperial Federation, then a hotly-debated topic as the increasing wealth of, and Britain's dependence on, the white dominions became more apparent:

Great Britain must therefore either sever herself completely from her Colonies, or else allow them a share in controlling the foreign policy of the Empire, and also in bearing the burden of maintaining the forces necessary to defend its coasts and commerce. If... we separate ourselves from our Colonies or allow them to separate from us, we shall be isolated in time of war, and liable in a moment to be starved out; so Great Britain will soon become a second- or third-class power. The lecturer closed with a passionate appeal to our patriotism, and the great future which lies before the Anglo-Saxon race, if they only combine and seize their opportunities now.

A lecture to the pupils in February 1896 by a Mr. H.V. Peatling was somewhat chaotic due to a missing magic lantern, but the message was clear. The Boers were singularly ungrateful, having allowed the British to defeat the Zulus for them and then declared independence. With 'considerable feeling' Mr. Peatling made clear his sympathies with Dr. Jameson and the Uitlanders, and ended with 'an appeal to our patriotism, to which all responded most heartily.' In the field of ecology, in 1899 a Mr. F.T. Bullen gave a talk to the school on 'Whales and Whale-Fishing', a detailed explanation of this now-unfashionable pursuit in which he had taken part as a crewman on an American whaler. The lecturer was very popular, 'electrifying his audience by an imitation of the weird cry which signifies that the man in the crow's nest has cited a whale, and graphically describing the successive operations of pursuit, capture, and bringing his carcass to the ship' not to mention 'describing the animal's death struggles.' In addition, 'he touched upon the great courage of whales, particularly of a cow-whale, which did not move while the blows of her captors were being rained upon her, since she feared to betray the presence of her calf beneath her sheltering fin.' Such lectures continued up to the outbreak of war: one on Australia was very well received in the spring of 1914.

This was all very well, but it was not quite military enough for the real enthusiasts. In the early days of Fettes, those boys who were impatient to go to war and whose aggression was not vented on the sports fields expressed themselves unofficially through the improvisation of firearms out of pieces of piping, the most impressive being William Oliver's 'twelve-inch Woolwich Infant' with which he 'used to bombard people from his study window as they were coming up from Glencorse.' In the 1870s, recalled the celebrated journalist George Campbell, 'the smell of gunpowder was strong in classrooms and passages.' The obituary of Neil MacVean, who died of fever contracted on service in the Boer War, mentioned that 'many O.F.s will remember how his face was pitted with blue marks – the result of incautiously looking down the barrel of a loaded gun.'

This continued until the immediate pre-war period; one pupil's memories of 1908 included the creation of bombs from stone ink-jars which were dropped from the roof of Carrington House. Prudently, the scientists who made them allowed classicists the pleasure of deploying the weapons, whilst fags were given the job of drying the gun-cotton made in the school laboratory. Hearing the explosions, the school steward 'declared poachers were in the grounds and demanded an escort.'

Even this was no substitute, fun though it was, for a more formal structure. The very first issue of the *Fettesian* carried 'an appeal to the martial spirits of Fettes' in the shape of a letter asking for a cadet corps. The correspondent said that he recognised there was the risk of enthusiasm dying out, but it would be worth a try, and would at any rate do something about the slouching for which the boys were constantly being told off.

The cadet movement had begun in 1860, partly influenced by the Cardwell reforms, the Crimean shock, and fears of invasion by Napoleon III (which also gave Britain coastal forts known as 'Palmerston's follies'). The first independent cadet unit is regarded as having been established by social reformer Octavia Hill in Southwark, ('the making of many a lad', as she put it) and various schools soon tried to set up their own bodies. Glenalmond soon had a corps, and Merchiston, the High School and the Academy (which had experimented with a drilling class in 1859) would all get one before Fettes.

Requests for a cadet corps were almost a hardy perennial in the pages of the school magazine, and became even more frequent around the time of the Boer War. 'Why should Fettes not have a rifle corps like the rest of our great public schools?' demanded a pupil in April 1899. 'Fettes, I am sorry to say, is practically the only Scottish Public School which does not possess a Volunteer Corps,' wrote another a couple of months later. The following year a lengthy piece appeared, which began:

Our country is at this moment plunged in war, and every one of her sons would like to help her in her present need. All the volunteers in the country are responding to the call to arms; and for ourselves, we witnessed a few days ago four of our former comrades respond to that call. Most of us, when we leave school, would like, if circumstances permitted, to be able to serve our country in a crisis such as this, but we find that one part of our training at school has been neglected. We find when we offer ourselves as volunteers we are rejected, because we know nothing of military drill, and are unaccustomed to the handling of a rifle.

This was somewhat disingenuous, as the Volunteers were full of OFs whose unmilitary schooling had presumably not been held against them. The writer promised that masters will not 'bear the drudgery and burden of the whole affair' – doubtless because plenty of masters had said that this would be precisely what would happen.

The school finally responded with an authorised statement in the magazine. The masters were, they said, worried about a decline of enthusiasm after initial interest – something which several of the pleading correspondents had indeed recognised as a potential problem – adding that this sort of thing had to be taken seriously, for 'he is no true friend to his country who plays at being a soldier'.

The staff common room was also aware that there was already a lot of compulsory activity at the school, so attempting to evade the problem of fluctuating interest (apparent in the rise and fall of the Debating Society) by making everyone join might be unpopular. They also pointed out that Fettes, after some controversy over the terms of its existence, the founder's will implying something rather different from the school as it actually was, was being left alone on the condition that it was giving the best possible academic education. Anything which interfered with this might drive down attainment and attract unwanted attention. They were, in any case, waiting to see what the government would do once the South African War was over.

Fettes' attitude of intellectual curiosity and determination to do one's best was something which the government hoped to make universal throughout the system, rather than being confined to a small number of respectable Scots whose role models were their housemasters. In addition to honing their skills on the pitch and in the classroom, the boys of Fettes had been arguing about all aspects of military, foreign and other policy for years. The first issue of the school magazine reported a debate on whether or not war was necessitated by British interests, and conscription itself was discussed in October 1878. Rowlatt (a keen debater who went on to become a distinguished judge), proposing that 'compulsory military service is desirable in England' (a distressingly frequent verbal slip to which Fettesians were all too prone at this time), argued that 'at present, it was the worst men who enlisted' and that if conscription was introduced people would get used to it as part of the natural course of things. He was supported by Hornsby, who pointed to the increasing global and treaty commitments of the country, and noted the strength of the German army – an early and unusual hostile reference to that nation. They were vigorously opposed by Bowden, who argued that 'the riff-raff of our large towns made splendid soldiers' and that both socialism and starving families would result from national service (as we have seen, he later became a conscientious vicar in New Zealand). Grindlay pointed out that the whole point of compulsory service was that it was compulsory, and would therefore apply to the tender plants of Fettes as well as to the aforesaid riff-raff. The motion was defeated, as it was again in 1882 and 1886, just as it was in cabinet, but the arguments remained in circulation for decades – interestingly, long before the National Service League made this a major issue of public debate in the aftermath of the Boer War.

Fettesians had a remarkable interest in these great affairs of the nation, and some of the debates were reported in great detail. A year after the conscription debate, and as a number of old boys were fighting there, the motion was 'that the present war with Afghanistan is unjustifiable.' Later that same year, the Society debated the fate of Sir Louis Cavagnari, the British Ambassador to Afghanistan, who on 3 September had been murdered along with dozens of his staff and soldiers, triggering the Second Afghan War, in which a number of Fettesians served.

Liberal motions were generally defeated, though in fairness not without their opponents, as in the case of the Ireland debate of October 1880 or women's suffrage in February 1881, having to make sophisticated cases. Modern Fettesians might disagree with young Fischer's point that 'women are impulsive and excitable, wanting in the judicial faculty, and both mentally and physically unfit for a part in political life.' With a certain music-hall timing, he added 'take Miss Parnell...' – a reference to the rabidly nationalist sister of the Home Rule leader Charles Stewart Parnell, who was privately embarrassed by her – and was rewarded with cries of 'No! No!' Other Victorian debates included a critique of the Short Service system, part of Cardwell's reforms, and one on the retention of flogging in the forces.

One intellectual theme which ran through the late nineteenth and early twentieth centuries is that of the desirability, on Darwinian grounds, of war in general and a titanic struggle between the nations in particular. It has even been argued that this contributed to the outbreak of war in 1914, a whole generation of young men having been indoctrinated with ideas of the desirability of struggle, and their leaders convinced of racial survival depending on the destruction of the country's rivals. These ideas were reflected in art, philosophy, literature and even psychology.

At a more particular level, the British popular press of the early twentieth century was awash with scare-stories about possible German invasion, France having been enthusiastically embraced by Edward VII and his Liberal ministers. There were now plenty of novels from the likes of William le Queux with titles such as *When William Came: A Story of London under the Hohenzollerns, Spies of the Kaiser* and *The Enemy in our Midst* which hypothesised about a Teutonic takeover. The *Daily Mail* even advertised such material by sending men dressed as German soldiers to march around London.

There is some evidence that a degree of notice was taken in the school of all of these influences. The *Fettesian* editorial for February 1886 was entitled 'Is the Human Race Degenerating?' a discussion of the views of the then prominent philosopher Herbert Spencer. 'The idea that the destructive effects of war were beneficial, that war cleansed and renewed society,' Hew Strachan observes, 'was one familiar to Social Darwinists. Both they and the younger generation of intellectuals were ready to welcome war as driving out decadence.'[69]

This was certainly an idea familiar to the Fettes College Debating Society. The debaters addressed the issue of war's benefits to mankind as early as 1879, with Bowden arguing that 'war was a great a beneficial purifying instrument when nations become corrupt, as in the case of Rome and Carthage. It was like the physician's knife which caused momentary pain but brought lasting benefits.' Against this, Lupton suggested that war was no more natural than disease, and, since it arose from 'the indulgence of the passions, we may say that it is not a necessity for the human race... as enlightenment spreads nations will cease to hate and make war on each other.' 'Ignorance of another country and its inhabitants' he said later, 'is often a cause of hatred of them... as knowledge spreads and intercourse increases, friendliness will spread too and wars will cease.'

The school library, where the Debating Society pondered the great issues of the day.

What is especially striking about these snapshots of Victorian thought at the school is that most boys rejected the notion of Social Darwinism; the editorial argued (influenced, it explained, by an article in the German magazine *Nord und Süd*) that the human race was not degenerating, but becoming bigger, stronger, healthier and longer-lived than before. Similarly, Bowden's motion lost heavily.

Such arguments continued up to the start of the war. A sardonic letter from Oxford in 1908 commented that the members of the University Officers' Training Corps 'hope to be efficient officers by the time of the German invasion – or Mr. le Queux's next novel on the subject.'

This tends to support, tiny cases though these are, Niall Ferguson's opposition to the notion that the intellectual climate of Europe from around 1870 'prepared men so well for war that they actually yearned for it.'[70] In the wider society, there was as much anti-militarism around as there was militarism. As Margaret MacMillan has noted in her recent study of the origins of the First World War, warfare was often seen as distasteful and outdated, especially the commercially-minded British, Americans and French. As the Debating Society showed, plenty of people supported the concept once proposed by the Enlightenment philosophers of eighteenth century Glasgow and Edinburgh that free trade, democracy, and better communication between states would bind the nations together in harmonious mutual self-interest.

That said, whilst the educated 'hearties' of the public schools might not uncritically have absorbed the more aggressive rhetoric of the period, they were still being trained in a broader set of values which would make them deeply loyal soldiers when the time came.

14. The Officers' Training Corps

Fettes' young ironsides were clearly excited by the army reforms which followed the Boer War, as they pointed towards some sort of role for the youthful volunteer as well as what the government optimistically hoped would be a more professional adult soldier. St John Broderick, the Tory War Minister, wanted to build up the army in terms of both size and equipment. For instance, the 'Long Lee' having been found unwieldy in South Africa, a more practical version was ordered, the .303 SMLE, less than four feet long, weighing less than nine pounds and with a ten-round magazine. Versions of this fine weapon would be used by Fettes cadets up to the present day (the No. 8 .22) whilst the descendants of the Indian soldiers and policemen trained by Victorian OFs can be seen using them against Maoist and Islamist troublemakers.

The Esher Committee reconstructed the army's 'brain' to ensure better organisation, and when the Tory government was ejected in the Liberal landslide of 1905, the extraordinarily gifted Scot R.B. Haldane, an alumnus of Fettes' rivals the Edinburgh Academy, took up the baton of reform. More than any of his predecessors, he had a vision, which the Fettes boys would have recognised, of the 'nation in arms':

...not a nation organized for jingo swagger; not a nation that desires fighting for fighting's sake; not a nation that holds a war lightly; but a nation that realizes the terrible nature of war, because its manhood knows what war means; a nation which is averse to strike the unless the blow to be called for in self-defence or in vindicating the cause of justice and righteousness.[71]

Working closely with his fellow-countryman, a professionally-minded young general called Douglas Haig, he set about creating a detailed training programme and a flexible, fully-equipped expeditionary force which could be sent overseas at short notice. He also reorganised the chaotic system of amateur county militias and volunteer units into the Territorial Army – a quarter of a million strong by 1910, and nicknamed (with some irony) the 'terrors'. He recognised that conscription, as demanded by Lord Roberts and the National Service League, was politically impossible in Britain and did not pursue it.

Linked to the creation of the Territorials was the idea of cadets at schools and universities to create a group of young men who would be ready to step in should the military need arise. Haldane envisaged that this would create, over a period of eight years, a body of several thousand potential officers, trained cheaply – the cost of the OTCs was around £150,000 per annum – and, in addition, ensuring that the student would render 'that service which the nation was entitled to expect from its manhood.'

The scheme offered a capitation fee of £1 per efficient cadet, with £10 for each one who gained a certificate and joined up, either as a regular or Territorial officer. The elaborate Scots uniform of the time cost around £3 each, and parents could contribute to this if they desired. Haldane faced criticism from both the left, who were simultaneously concerned about the militarization of education and reliance on the public schools, and the right, who accepted that things had to change but were not sure how.

Nonetheless, committed to the OTC as a central (and cheap) plank in the building of 'the nation in arms', bringing the army and the public (or at least upper-middle-class boys) together, Haldane toured the country in the late 1900s, encouraging and promoting his creation – to the extent that, after opening yet another OTC at Reading in 1909, he wrote that 'it is a great bore to do those things, but they have to be done.' Haldane's vision for his cadets was clear; without the unBritish, illiberal and expensive expedient of mass conscription:

>...it is not too much to expect that, in the event of the supreme national emergency, feelings of patriotism would, as has always been the case in the past, induce a certain number of gentlemen to come forward and take commissions...many of whom would have had the advantage of the improved training given in the Officers' Training Corps.[72]

Professor Hew Strachan has commented that 'popular enthusiasm played no part in causing the First World War. And yet without a popular willingness to go to war the world war could not have taken place.'[73] Fettes reflected that willingness when, at long last, it embarked upon the military training for which so many boys had yearned for so long. Shooting began as a school sport five years after the Boer War ended, with a creation of a miniature rifle range in the gymnasium, a fact recorded in the 1907 'Vive-la' commemorating the year's events:

We've a deadly machine which would please Mr Haldane
Set up in this Gym – but it's carefully walled-in.

The technical marvels of the range – its concrete floor, glass roof, rails for retrieving targets and bullet-catchers – were lovingly described in the *Fettesian* to an admiring readership. A rifle club was formed and a shooting team went to Bisley for the first time in 1908, possibly inspired by the fact that this was the year of the first London Olympics, when Britain won 147 medals, three times as many as the USA, which came second.

Boys being boys, there was to be a lengthy correspondence in the pages of the *Fettesian* about shooting colours, which initially consisted of a hat-band – 'of remarkably little use to anyone: for who is going to wear a straw hat in the winter term?' Subsequent letters complained about the 'grotesque and unintelligible hieroglyphic' on the hat-bands, and another simply damned the fact that 'so manly a sport should be represented by so effeminate a token'.

The (eventually) improved colours aside, shooting alone was not quite good enough for the true enthusiasts, and so, following Lord Roberts' 'appeal to youth' and incentives from the government, in November 1908 Fettes established an Officers' Training Corps, with Mr. T.B. Franklin as Officer Commanding and John Hay Beith ('a gentle but firm disciplinarian, who was immensely popular') as Company Officer. Neither 'spared themselves, nor those under them, in promoting efficiency'.

The school's motives were not entirely altruistic: if OTC membership was now going to be expected of a lad hoping to become an army officer, then Fettes needed to provide it if it was to continue competing in this market. Watson's and Heriot's, whose staff had had similar doubts, also signed up at this point. The *Fettesian* announced the new body's creation with pride in November 1908:

Fettes is at last in possession of a Cadet Corps, and, on the principle that one volunteer is worth ten pressed men, it is highly satisfactory to note that no compulsion of any kind was required to fill the ranks to overflowing.

Our establishment is to consist of a Company of one hundred. No less than 137 volunteers came forward in response to the Headmaster's appeal – practically all the eligible members of the School, in fact – with the result that many excellent candidates had to be rejected. However, a 'reserve squad' has been formed, which, though 'off the strength', will serve as a very valuable feeding-force to the Company as vacancies occur.

Parades have been proceeding briskly since the beginning of October, and already squad drill has been sufficiently mastered to make it possible to form a Company. There has also been some simple skirmishing, and many embryo warriors have received their first lesson in the art of taking cover – in the Fettes pond...

The Corps was divided into four house sections, and devoted itself to drill once a week until it had 'lost the appearance of a football crowd which had suddenly found itself in unaccustomed groups.' By the end of its first few months, an unidentified reporter could note that, although 'a somewhat trying time', it had been 'an excellent term's work, characterised all through by a keenness which augurs well for the efficiency of the company next term.'

In the absence of uniforms and significant numbers of rifles, much of the early cadet activity revolved around square-bashing, which 'though very necessary, is hardly exciting' and the 'lack of rifles, ammunition and uniforms gives the impression that it is not quite the real thing.' The existence of the Shooting VIII, and inter-house competitions, however, gave the new cadets something to aim for. College, the scholarship boys in the main building, won the first Efficiency Cup in 1908 with 90 points out of a possibly 110 (Carrington got 83, Glencorse 77 and Moredun with Kimmerghame 75).

Uniforms and weapons arrived early in 1909, on the pattern of Scottish regiments of the time with khaki tunics, Glengarry caps and kilts. The first Senior Cadet Officer was Norman Macleod Adam, and the hunting version of the Macleod tartan was accordingly adopted for the cadets' kilts. Training became steadily more intense with lectures on tactics, attack and defence schemes and a full dress parade in February 1909.

That spring, Lord Rosebery allowed them to use Dalmeny Park for exercises, and soon they were in a position to hold a field-day on Corstorphine Hill against Edinburgh Academy; they seized the enemy's position through the clever use of a holding attack on the left flank and then a real one on the right. Unfortunately, the subsequent attempt to fight a rearguard action as they retreated downhill cost Fettes many 'casualties'.

The umpires decided 'that our first attack was carefully screened, well delivered and entirely successful' but the retreat demonstrated 'slowness of retiring, and lack of covering fire.' This reckless bravery and unwillingness to retreat had already characterised those OFs who had perished in combat, and would be readily apparent in the coming years.

The *Fettesian* was boundlessly enthusiastic, editorialising at the end of the OTC's first year that it 'had been taken up in the right spirit and thoroughly mastered'; the Headmaster's Founder's Day speech not only praised the teachers who led it but addressed 'the importance of putting the country in the right state of mind as well as the right state of body.' Founder's Day also featured the innovation of a cadet march past and bugle call, and the 'Vive-la' had an unprecedented two verses on the corps:

Of late we have startled the tax-payer frugal
By the rattle of arms and the blare of the bugle,
And the mothers of Stockbridge have trembled with dread
At the sound of our volleys – though minus the lead.

For to add to his 'terrors' a flavour that's Spartan
Mr. Haldane has dressed us in khaki and tartan,
And he'll surely be cheered in the midst of his trouble
To see Mr. Franklin come up at the double.

The first year of the Fettes cadet corps finished on something of an anti-climax, for owing to an outbreak of measles the boys could not attend a summer camp. However, by the following March, they were taking part in an elaborate exercise at West Calder alongside the Edinburgh University OTC (including, excitingly, their artillery and machine-gun) against the Academy and George Watson's College. Although impressed by their enemies' bravery – they 'retired with a disregard for personal danger which would have been very admirable had we been supplied with ball-cartridge, but in actual warfare they would have been wiped out' – the Fettesians were still delighted when Mr. Franklin led a charge which forced the enemy back 'in utmost disorder' leaving Dalmahoy Hill 'covered in a gesticulating crowd of Watsonians, still indignant at the rough usage they had received'. The umpire, 'mystified by the widely divergent reports of the rival officers, refused to give any decision' but this did nothing to spoil 'an instructive and enjoyable day'.

That summer, Pte. Tommy Stout put up an appropriately robust show at Bisley in appalling weather; also a successful rugby player, he was to die at Gallipoli in 1915, rescuing a superior officer. Mr. Franklin gained useful insights by spending part of his 1909 holidays conducting military research, with Wellington College at Christmas and at Easter shadowing the army's preparations against a possible invasion of Dunbar. Finding the exercise director's car, containing a picnic with several bottles of beer, he and a colleague helped themselves in true soldierly scavenger fashion. 'No mention was made of the theft,' he remembered on his retirement, 'but that evening, when our papers were returned, we found written across our solutions in red pencil – "this scheme shows signs of alcoholic confusion." Field glasses are evidently useful like on occasion for other than military purposes.'

The Glencorse House section of the OTC in 1909

The school's early concern about cadet activities interfering with school study was not, apparently, without foundation, for in 1910 a warning had to be issued that reading and revision for the important 'Certificate A' examination (essential for quick advancement as an officer in the army) had to be done out of school hours. This was taken extremely seriously by the boys who sat it – more proof, if it were needed, of the Fettes determination to 'get things right' – the March 1913 *Fettesian* carried both a review of a useful revision guide to this exam (written by Captain Franklin himself) and a poem, 'Dulce et Decorum est pro Patria Mori':

I saw a youth at break of day,
Who toiled with pick and shovel.
He dug a trench three feet each way,
And straight within did grovel.
But out he sprang with look of pain,
'By Jove! I quite forgot the drain.'
'Why do you thus? Pray tell me, pray!'
'I'm working hard for Certificate A.'

In 1914 an incentive system was introduced as for boys to make greater efforts; seven points were needed to get a special silver badge, and could be gained for efficiency (one point), Certificate A Oral (two points), Certificate A Written (three points), shooting (one point), winning a competition (one point) or attending camp (two points).

The first summer camp attended by the Fettes cadets was in late July 1910 at Blair Atholl, 'a vast field of mud, covered with what looked like a crop of large dingy-white mushrooms' in which, despite being prepared 'for all kinds of hardships' the boys slept 'in pools of water and shockingly bad tempers.' Awoken at 5.30 'by a confused sound which might have been anything from the expiring effort of a domestic cock to the plaintive trumpeting of a dyspeptic elephant' but was in fact a bugler with a sore throat, they embarked on a programme of marching which was cut short by a torrential downpour. The next day's field exercise might have been a military success, 'but it could hardly be described as enjoyable'; 'lying flat on your stomach in wet heather, and feeling the moisture gradually penetrate your uniform till it reaches your shivering skin, is certainly a novel sensation, but it is not a pleasant one.' The authorities decided to strike camp and on the Sunday the boys returned to Edinburgh, where they marched from Haymarket station to the school, 'a strange spectacle', for since their uniforms were too wet to wear they had on a strange assortment of pyjamas and rugby socks beneath their greatcoats and glengarries. 'We look back on camp as on a bad dream' concluded the *Fettesian* reporter.

Subsequent camps were rather more successful; Barry in 1911 was sunny and allowed for both drill and realistic exercises, though the reporter noted with envy that other schools had bands. This was soon to be rectified with the creation of a pipe band in 1912; it took fourth place at the camp competition that year, despite the fact that its existence had been 'a mystery' throughout the camp (no-one having seen it). Admittedly, there were only five schools at the camp that (again, very wet) year, but it must have been a great comfort to Fettes that on their first outing they had beaten one of them.

Needless to say, schoolboy perversity ensured that no sooner had the pipe band they so desired been established than 'scathing sarcasms and invidious innuendoes' were levelled at the musicians. Nonetheless, it was to attract considerable attention at church parades and other public events. By the 1913 camp, it had been given £100 by Old Fettesians to support the purchase of uniforms and instruments, and came third in the competition, being singled out for praise by an officer for both appearance and efficiency.

The pipe band at camp; this picture was taken shortly after the First World War but its ceremonial uniform has been unchanged since 1912

Memories of the period vary considerably. George Gillen was enthusiastic about his time as a cadet; some years later, he recalled the battle on Corstorphine Hill in 1909 'where the new Corps fought with great élan and some skill', although 'a laudable attempt to give greater fire effect by the insertion of BB shot in blank cartridges was not, however, looked on with favour.' The nature of the cadet corps' activities can be seen from his memories of a combined field day at Dumyat Hill on June 15 of that year:

The Corps entrained at Waverley, after marching down to the strains of J.M. MacDonald's pipes, and put in a full day's work under more or less service conditions. It does not seem to have suffered from the unaccustomed strain of carrying rifles and full cartridge belts (and full haversacks) for many hours, as it attacked uphill in the afternoon with an impetuosity which called forth loud (but scarcely admiring) protests from the umpires.

He remembered with some pride that at their first formal inspection, a mere ten months after the unit was established, the Inspecting Officer considered the results of the training reflected 'great credit on all concerned' and that 11 per cent of his contemporaries joined the army. 46 out of 53 members of the class of 1905 joined the armed forces, but the register suggests that most did so on the outbreak of war rather than on leaving school – only five are definitely known to have left Fettes and begun a military career in peacetime. (By contrast, six out of the 35 boys of 1878 became professional soldiers, a higher proportion.)

Of the 1905 class, 25 joined the infantry (mostly in Scots regiments), and seven the Artillery; small numbers joined the Engineers, the Royal Navy, the Royal Army Service Corps, and the RAF; two went into the Indian Army, one as a cavalryman. Nine were killed. Of the boys from that period who did not serve, most had died of illness or accident before they could join up. Fifteen OFs of the 1906 cohort were killed, and the same number for 1907, with another dying in peacetime as a result of his wounds. All but three of the 1910 class also served, and 19 died.

Not all of the boys were so fascinated by cadet life. A. Murray Stephen said the OTC 'was accepted without great enthusiasm at first and was regarded as an amusing novelty.' So far as he was concerned, there was 'a naturally sloppy look of a half-grown boy fitted out in a stock-sized Army kilt and hung around with unaccustomed trappings'; 'I can remember the overloaded feeling of everything being a size too big for my immature frame.' His recollections of cadet life were of a Royal Inspection in Windsor Great Park when, after a twelve-hour train journey, they were drawn up with a strong summer sun beating down on them, and 'one after another the smaller boys pitched forward, until we were faced another way.' Mr. Franklin recalled afterwards that:

We were to be inspected almost last, and men were fainting right and left in the other schools. As yet none of us had fallen out, but at last a man in the front rank swayed... disgrace imminent... But his near rank man with admirable presence of mind and callousness, jabbed his bayonet point into the back of the man's knee and drew blood. The swaying stopped.

The Windsor event was the first official public appearance of the OTC as a body, 20,000 strong, from schools and universities across Britain, and the *Fettesian* covered it enthusiastically, noting that the 'swinging sporrans and flashing accoutrements' of the Scottish contingents were popular both with spectators and royals, and that the martyrs to heatstroke had not fallen in vain, because it meant everyone was allowed to sit down. The King's warm message to Minister for War Haldane was reported with pride:

It points with no uncertain hand to the existence of that 'individual efficiency' by which nowadays we rightly set so much store, and which is only achieved by unfaltering keenness, unquestioning obedience to discipline, and cheerful compliance with what are very often tiresome and monotonous conditions. In that great camp we are proud to state that Fettes and Loretto were especially singled out for praise in this respect. That is a good beginning for a permanent tradition.

Loretto, incidentally, had its own eccentric tradition; in keeping with the strictures about rational dress of its great headmaster Almond, its corps wore open-necked shirts and slouch hats. They thus escaped, legend has it, the suffering of the Fettes cadets in the blazing sun.

For all the delight that the Corps took in the admiring comments of captains and kings, undoubtedly the praise which meant most to the boys was from 'the Sarge'. Like many schools, Fettes employed a succession of former army sergeants to teach physical education, and the longest-serving and best-loved of these was P. Adam, formerly of the Scots Guards. In 1911 he gave an interview to the *Fettesian* in which he described his experiences in the Crimea, where he had fought at Alma, Balaclava, Inkerman and Sebastopol, and told the boys that the cadets were 'doing jolly well. Sometimes when I see you start out for a field day I just wish that I could go along with you: but my old bones are getting stiff with rheumatism.'

Another great role model for the boys was Old Fettesian Major Mieklejohn, VC, who was also a supporter of the cadet movement. Before the Great War, Meiklejohn visited the school, where this 'modest and inspiring hero' made a great impression. Although he was not very eloquent and made no mention of his valiant actions at Elandslaagte, he spoke of doing one's job, and the kind of public service that a school like Fettes could and did perform on the young. The young Robert Bruce Lockhart left the assembly 'with a new determination in my heart to do my own job better than I had done it before.'[74]

This good resolution lasted all of twenty-four hours. Meiklejohn lasted only a little longer. In 1913 he was at a parade in Hyde Park when his horse bolted, straight for some women and children; he tried steering it away, which was difficult owing to his having lost an arm, and he was impaled on a fence at Rotten Row; 'in this last desperate act of gallantry both mare and rider were killed.' The school was distraught. A fund was set up to establish a memorial to him (placed in the school chapel a few months before war broke out) and to educate his three children. The *Fettesian* obituary concluded:

Sad as is the premature removal of so distinguished a Fettesian, and deeply as we sympathise with his bereaved relations, we cannot but feel pride in the courage and heroism that marked his life no less than his death. His example cannot fail to inspire not only those among us who are going to be soldiers, but all who aspire to do good work in the world and show themselves brave men.

15. The Last Year of Peace

What is rather surprising about the *Fettesians* of the immediate pre-war years is the relative absence, in comparison with those of the Victorian and Edwardian eras, of significant interest in current affairs. The 1909-12 *Fettesians* represent a kind of pre-war peak of topical debates and references. A satirical interpretation of the *Daily Express* editorial 'Tariff Reform means goals for all' had supposed quotes from other sources about how our national games would be 'more in accordance with modern civilisation' if each side could choose its 'own time and manner for kicking goals'. There were also letters from worthy bodies and individuals exhorting the boys to join, for instance, the Agenda Club (which hoped to involve school- and university-leavers in a kind of voluntary service among the disadvantaged) the Red Cross and, of course, Lord Roberts, who wrote a blanket letter to schoolboys in 1912:

> You have had great advantages as British public schoolboys, and as British citizens you will have even greater privileges. What do you mean to give your country in return? It is in the power of every one of you to give personal service, that is, deliberately to work for your nation as well as for yourself; but personal service means some sacrifice of self, the giving up of some leisure and of some amusement. At the present time your personal service is needed to persuade your fellow-countrymen of the great necessity there is for every able-bodied man being trained to defend his country in time of need.

The Debating Society was, as always, the first port of call for the boy who, in addition to training to fight for his country, wanted to discuss how it worked. A 1909 debate on Lloyd George's 'People's Budget' was marred by J.M. Benson's 'personal attacks upon the character and antecedents of the Budget, and he had to be called to order' (this debate was followed up by a poem in which manful attempts were made to find rhymes with 'Budget' – 'grudge it' and 'judge it' were achieved).

In 1910, there were some truly excellent debates on the House of Lords – then at the centre of a constitutional scandal for their attempts to meddle in the celebrated Budget – and Tariff Reform. The following year, the Debating Society covered Ireland; Gordon, future pilot of renown, proposed that Home Rule 'compatible with the supremacy of the British Parliament, be granted to Ireland' and R.A. Hendy, later to be killed in the post-war 'troubles' there, was in the chair. The motion, before 'a strongly prejudiced audience' lost by four to 25.

The Debating Society seems to have become a bit rickety at this point; after some ill-tempered and poor-quality debates in the winter of that, J.A.G. Leask, later to win the MC in France, wrote in his report for the *Fettesian* that it 'has had a somewhat precarious existence for some time, but it is to be feared that this crowning disgrace will prove its death-blow.' There was one final flaring of discussion of the great events of the day in the spring of 1912, when a passionate and often clever debate took place on the trustworthiness of the government, followed up by a witty bout between two of the masters on the subject of tipping, but thereafter the debaters' consideration of great events disappears from the pages of the *Fettesian* – but then, as Leask noted regretfully in the final report, 'what can one say of a Society whose Secretary appears late, and in bedroom slippers?'

This is not, of course, to say that with the collapse of the Debating Society the boys completely lost all curiosity about the world beyond the iron railings. It is true, for instance, that they followed the career of Sir John Simon, probably the most politically successful OF until Tony Blair, as he progressed through the Liberal ranks and occupied posts such as representative of the Board of Trade in the *Titanic* Inquiry. But such interest was always variable. William McClure recalled that the main reasons he read the *Saturday Review* in the 1890s were George Bernard Shaw and J.F. Runciman, the newspaper's cultural critics, rather than the world news – and he became a journalist. The 1913 'Vive-la' reference to the Balkan wars in the context of games was about the limit of current affairs coverage:

The XI, we feared, would be made to play Turkey
To Academy's Servia and the Bulgars of Merchi

It would be hard to tell, looking at copies of the school magazine for 1913, that the civil peace of the United Kingdom was threatened by anarcho-syndicalist agitation in Wales, the Suffragette campaign (which saw Fettes' upper classroom set on fire) and, most disturbingly, Ireland's split into two armed camps which were ready to fight over Home Rule.

There were Fettesians on both sides of this conflict: the OFs who were Liberal MPs supported Home Rule, as did the Barton brothers of Glendalough. However, most were hostile, and at least one, William Lenox-Conyngham (whose brother George returned to Fettes as a master) was a senior officer in the Ulster Volunteer Force. Lenox-Conyngham had a distinguished military career, and was decorated in the Boer War; like many Ulstermen, he opposed Home Rule and made the family home, Springhill, a centre of UVF activity, hosting a grand meeting with Sir Edward Carson. He was commander of the South Londonderry Regiment of the UVF and his wife organized a network of eleven field hospitals for the organization, all in readiness for a civil war which never came. The *Fettesian* reported his appointment blandly in its news of 'The Services' in November 1913, between S.G.M. Smith's promotion to the chair of political economy at Lucknow University and Sir John Simon's acceptance of the Liberal candidacy of North-West Manchester for an election which was expected to take place the following year.

A letter from an OF in the army, sent to the school 'from an outpost' on the North-West Frontier that autumn, concerned not great world events but the trials and tribulations of introducing association football to the Indian Army. Apparently Sikhs did not take very well to it because of their turbans ('a circumstance which naturally is not conducive to accurate heading') and preferred hockey, for which they had 'a fine natural eye.' The Gurkha was an excellent soccer-player, although 'arms were freely used for forbidden purposes, usually with more skill than the player exhibited with his foot.' An article intriguingly entitled 'Shakespeare on the game' also turned out, perhaps disappointingly, to have been about sport, one of a number of pastiches which the magazine regularly printed.

Less cheerfully, there was a sad, perfunctory death notice for the unfortunate Charles Ralph Warwick, who had left the school a mere five years previously and died in the sinking of the *Empress of Ireland* in the St Lawrence, which with over a thousand fatalities was almost as great a disaster as the *Titanic* two years earlier (on which George Lenox-Conyngham's wife and children had travelled as far as Cherbourg).

The *Fettesians* for the last summer of peace in 1914 mentioned Henry Hamilton Fyfe's new book on the Ulster crisis, but did not review it. In June, the retirement from the Indian Civil Service of patriarch J.C. Arbuthnott was reported: his intellect, devotion to duty, command of native languages and uprightness of character were all praised, as was his unerring aim and dedication to hunting ('none but himself can say how many tiger, elephant and rhino have fallen to his rifle'). There was poetry about golf and cricket, poetry about the weather, and poetry about poetry. There seems to have been an increase in Corps activity, and there was poetry about that. There was a lengthy effort about the landscape target, a large painting of countryside which was used to instruct cadets (and indeed all trainee soldiers) in identifying features in the countryside. Part of this reads:

The enemy had now attacked a field
Wherein a solitary haystack stood:
From there extended down towards a wood
They held (the rhyme demands the word) the weald.

Then they advanced across the bright green ground,
By squads and sections by the purple burn;
My knees were loosened and I tried to turn,
I could but drop and quake behind a mound.

This dream sequence based on the target would have raised a wry smile from many generations of those trained in this way by the British Army; versions are still in use today.

There were several field days, events which were becoming increasingly elaborate with a thousand cadets from Edinburgh's schools taking part in the biggest ones. On 18 March, the Corps detrained at Glencorse station to take part in an exercise in the Pentland hills against Loretto. Fettes represented the state of Penicuik, and their goal was to dislodge some troops of the rival state of Currie, said to be raiding cattle – not wholly different from the role of the former pupil who wrote from his outpost on the Indian frontier. The training was hard enough – cadets had to descend near-perpendicular hills, wade through icy rivers up to their kilted knees, struggle through bogs, and even contend with a snowstorm. A masterly flank attack organized by a Lance-Corporal from Schoolhouse 'surprised and annihilated' the enemy, giving Fettes the victory, and they returned to Glencorse barracks, tired, wet, but fairly contented. As the reporter put it, 'the horrors of war were brought home to us, not so much by hails of 'blank' as by the difficulties attending the advance and the hostility of the elements.'

This does not mean that they were ready to face a real enemy; the report of the 25 May field day refers to a colossal map-reading error which doubled the length of their march, and a bayonet charge covered by 'desultory' covering fire, which the umpires declared a failure. The man from the War Office who inspected the cadets on 8 July was impressed by the 'efficient and well-turned out' pipe band, the keen officers, useful signallers and good marching, but also noticed that 'a good many cadets wanted their hair cut' and that during the exercise 'there was a good deal of laughing and talking' which 'rather spoiled the whole thing.'

The absence of military or political content in the school magazines or memoirs of former pupils in 1913-14 appears surprising to us, but only because of the cataclysm which we know lay just around the corner. They did not know this (by contrast, there is a mounting tension, with many references to fascism and exhortations to join the Territorial Army, visible in copies of the *Fettesian* in the thirties). Whilst the war planners of the great powers were often feverishly excited in those years, the average member of the public, outside the Balkans, was not aware of the threat of war. Old Fettesians were less likely to be shot at in 1913 or early 1914 than they were in 1900. Even politicians were more sanguine than they were in 1939. 'There is no such thing as an inevitable war,' said Bonar Law, 'If war comes it will be from a failure of human wisdom.'

As for the domestic troubles, the school wanted to avoid controversy. The suffragettes who burned the upper were to be denied the oxygen of publicity, and Ulster was an even more flammable subject in Scotland. Despite – or because of – the close family ties many boys and masters had with it, the powder-keg next door was a no-go area for the school magazine. It would be interesting to speculate what the boys of Kimmerghame House would have made of the UVF gun-running of their housemaster's brother, or indeed what the Debating Society (had it existed) would have made of any of the great political events of 1912-14. In a sense, though, this does not matter. The core curriculum emphasizing hard work, physical courage, and devotion to duty – this remained in place regardless of political awareness, and enabled the latest generation of Fettesians to 'do their bit' with the Victorians when war broke out.

There is confirmation of the folk-memory of a glorious summer in 1914 in the pages of the *Fettesian*: the rule that Sports Day weather was 'notoriously unpleasant' was broken, a welcome relief after a spring term disrupted by a measles epidemic. Although a couple of matches were rained off towards the end of term, on Founder's Day itself 'the sun shone out' for the festivities. These included the traditional speeches and prize-giving, a concert of music and drama (repeated later for the residents of the local poor-house) and a cricket match against an Old Fettesian team. Founder's Day took place on 27 June 1914, the day before the assassination of the Archduke Franz Ferdinand by a Serbian student the same age as the sixth formers at Fettes.

The only inkling of what was to come was the note that although there was a large gathering of Old Fettesians, there were 'perhaps not quite so many as used to gather in before camps and training corps became common.' The 'Vive-La' contained its usual blend of school news, former pupils' achievements and excruciating rhymes:

Old Fettesian honours we're proud to narrate,
For Simon now sits on the Council of State,
And we gladly now offer to Jardine a due salaam
Just appointed a Knight of St. John at Jerusalem.

To the East there is really a wonderful exodus –
We've 'heard it a-calling' – it's fairly annexed us –
While Smith at Lucknow holds the Chair of Economy
At Hong-Kong David Landale holds office with bonhomie.

And with Davidson starting to govern in India
There's no fear Baboo shindies will ever grow shindier,
And if Egypt grows traitors they'll vanish with speed
When tackled all round by Blair, Purves and Reid.

To the Army we've sent of our best as before,
For Miller has sailed to the land of Tagore,
While Glegg's earned his place in an Indian Brigade,
And Moir into Sandhurst a sudden sprint made.

There was some sorrow because the revered groundsman, Geordie Howell, was retiring: 'He seemed an institution, not a mortal, but an immortal.' On the whole, though, the day was a delightful one, with warm remarks from the chairman of the governors, who referred to the death, the previous year, of Major Meiklejohn VC, in whose honour a memorial tablet had gone up in chapel, and expressed his pleasure at the flourishing state of the Corps. Fettesians had, as boys do, recovered from the saddest event of 1914, the sudden death of Patrick Sellar on 26 February in Malcolm House, the school's sanatorium. The measles he had contracted during the epidemic which had blighted the spring term's sports had been supervened by pneumonia. Aged sixteen and a half, and tipped as a possible Head of School, 'his cheerful, kindly nature, his quick sense of humour and his quiet personal charm had endeared him to many who will long mourn the loss of a personal friend.'

They must surely have imagined that this would be the full extent of the tragedies they would encounter; the robustness of youth ensured that the issue of the magazine which followed the one with Sellar's obituary carried a poem, 'On not being allowed to the International: a complaint', bemoaning the school's refusal to let pupils attend the Calcutta Cup, in which two old boys were playing. Although they were different times, and there was something of a Fettes tradition of writing poems about contagious disease (two appeared in one issue of the magazine after a flu epidemic in the early 1900s), more sensitive twenty-first century readers might consider it a little tasteless to print a poem which included verses like this so soon after a boy's death:

'You must battle with bacilli' – 'tis the warcry of mankind –
'You must keep the scarlet scourge outside your door,
And engage in single combat with the largest mump you find
Or a melee with a measle on the floor.'

To the modern reader, there is a poignancy about these last peacetime copies of the school magazine, with their cheerful optimism. The July 1914 number was full of fun. Alfred le Maitre wrote a loving, though self-deprecating, eulogy to his cricket bat, 'Chips', and the Head of School himself contributed a 'Dictionary' to help people understand Fettesian 'terms of purely local interest'. These included prefect ('a big man with a raucous voice'), fag ('a small man, blind, deaf, and often of grimy appearance. Breaks ornaments and has no capacity for lighting fires'), and prep ('a time provided by the authorities for recreation'). There was news of former pupils: six had married, and two were now proud fathers. 'The Services' were defined broadly: in addition to news that Moodie and McCosh had received army promotions, OFs' appointments in the worlds of imperial administration, medicine, teaching, and the church were included. There were reviews of *The Public Schools Cricket Year Book* and Fettes' own Captain Franklin's *Tactics and the Landscape*. There are letters to the editor urging the adoption of the cello by the school orchestra and the repair of the College clock, a topic which was something of a hardy perennial in the *Fettesian*.

The magazine carried its traditional detailed sports reports, with elaborate tables of batting averages, scores for each team, bowling analysis and long descriptions of matches - Glencorse v. Carrington took up a page and a half of close type. Cricket, wrote Mr. Cumberledge, 'generally is certainly in a healthy and flourishing condition, even if outstanding individual excellence is somewhat lacking.' The 1st XI had won seven, lost six and drawn five matches, though the future did not look rosy since the under-fifteen team had lost all but two matches, one of which was against a prep school. 'A rather sluggish and unpolished lot,' concluded Cumberledge. The last peacetime *Fettesian* contained an anonymous poem, 'The Magic of the Sun', part of which reads:

There is a field across the way
Where, on a shining summer day,
I looked and saw Demeter stand,
With sheaves and poppies in her hand.

But now, e'en though I stand and wait
From early dawn till twilight late
Nothing is there at eve or morn
But poppies growing mid the corn.

To the boy who wrote this, poppies were simply flowers which grew in fields; within a few years, and thanks to another poem, they would be a symbol of something else entirely. It is hard to read those lines now and not be reminded of the folk-songs about the Somme which began to appear in the seventies.

By the time the magazine was printed and posted (200 of the 1500 copies to former pupils going overseas), the Archduke Franz Ferdinand was dead, and his close friend Kaiser Wilhelm of Germany had given a 'blank cheque' to Vienna to retaliate. Every schoolboy knows what happened next. And yet there had been trouble in the Balkans before, and many Britons assumed that Serbia, which had been something of a 'rogue state' and with which the Empire had few ties, would be punished for being such a nuisance. Alfred le Maitre remembered that, whilst the murder of the Archduke was undoubtedly noticed, 'on the whole, like most healthy people, we didn't worry very much. The possibility of a war had never been very far away from us, and most of these political businesses got smoothed over one way or the other.'

The teachers, however, sensed something in the air. William Adam recalled a sad little remark by his housemaster, in that first week of July, to one of the war's many innocent victims:

...during the last week of term the serenity of its passage was disturbed by the touch of a cold shadow. On the Sunday night, when leaving K. P.'s room, the boy immediately in front of me – the youngest in the house and son of the naturalized German consul at Sunderland – paused in saying good-night, and K. P. remarked that it looked as if we would be at war with Germany in a few days. Within a fortnight Ahlers' father had been arrested for 'communicating with the enemy' and had been condemned to be shot. Later he was reprieved, but his family suffered great privations.

Herbert Ahlers' father Nicholas had, in fact, been arranging for his countrymen to return home when war was declared, in the sure knowledge that they would be called to the German colours, and the case attracted the attention of both the *New York Times* and the House of Lords. He was found guilty under a treason statute of Edward III, but the case was quashed by the Court of Appeal. The family lived under an assumed name in Surbiton until it was discovered that they were receiving £10 each month from Germany via Holland; Nicholas Ahlers was interned. The strain affected Nicholas' wife Emma deeply: highly-strung and addicted to veronal, she was herself interned, and committed suicide in Holloway Prison in 1917. Although Herbert's older brother Edgar joined the army (attesting in khaki to his loyalty at their mother's inquest) the family seems to have been deported after the war.

The last day of term proceeded as normal with prizegiving in the gym; Adam won his for Middle School Maths. Looking back many years later, he wrote:

The Cloud gathering on the European horizon and did not cast its shadow over the end-of-term festivities, and that night there was the 'House Pop' in the tea-room at Glencorse, with several O.F.s down to join us, a good 'groise' (i.e. feast) and a sing-song.

But after the Cloud came the Storm. Within a week war had been declared and the Old Order had vanished. Of those present that night, who were subsequently old enough to see active service, one-fifth had been killed before the signing of the Armistice. The school generation immediately before that of my first term suffered still worse with a toll as high as one-third. Gone were thoughts of careers in the professions, in the civil services, in business, or in the management of family estates; to those leaving school there was now only one sequel – War, on the land, on the sea, or in the air.

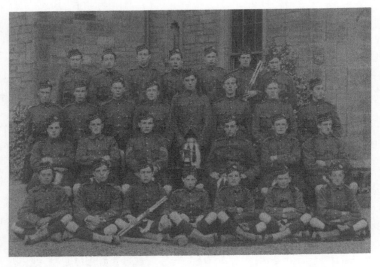

The Moredun section of the OTC in 1913; a third were killed and a third injured

Epilogue

Around a thousand Fettesians served in the armed forces in the Great War, and a quarter died; the youngest still in their teens, the oldest, Major Denis Macpherson, cut down by machine-gun fire leading his men into battle at Loos, aged 53.

Of the 36 pupils who left the school that summer, 14 would be killed in the war - the first, Stephen Williamson, winner of prizes for swimming and essays, a keen sportsman, destined for a place at Oxford, fell at Neuve Chapelle on 10 March 1915, still aged 18, only nine months after Founder's Day. His friend Malcolm Maclean, another prefect in College, 'a big forward, good out of touch, who works hard in the scrum', died later that year at Loos. Three of the four winners of Upper Sixth Governors' Prizes were killed: Mackay (Greek iambics), Mackinnon (Greek prose), and Robertson (Latin hexameters and prose). The fourth, le Maitre (English poem) was severely wounded. Of the Men In Authority - heads of house, team captains and cadet NCOs - half were killed. John Mackay, the Head of School, winner of a classical scholarship to Oxford, died on 20 August 1917 of wounds received on 31 July, the opening day of the Battle of Passchendaele.

Eric Templeton Young, the Old Fettesian who made his debut for Scotland at Inverleith in the match the Fettes boys could not attend because of measles, was one of six former pupils killed in a Turkish attack at Helles on 28 June 1915. Four of them had been in Glencorse together in the mid-1900s. Indeed, more Glencorsians died in the war (71) than are currently members of the house, despite the school's great expansion since 1914.

Between its opening and the outbreak of war, Fettes had produced 37 rugby internationals; the oldest were in their fifties in 1914 but everyone who could join up did so. At least 19 Fettesians who had played rugby for Scotland served in the First World War; six died. These included the great David Bedell-Sivright, killed by septicemia in the Dardanelles, and John Argentine Campbell, so hero-worshipped in his day. He represented Cambridge at rugby, cricket, and athletics, was capped for Scotland, taught for a time at Loretto, then returned to Argentina where his team won the national polo championship. When war broke out, he wrote to a team-mate asking to be excused from the forthcoming match:

I have just heard that war is declared between England and Germany. Although possibly it may seem foolish, I would prefer not to play public polo while our people are at it over there; so I hope you will allow me to stand out. I feel that if one can go in for games at this time we shouldn't be here but should be on the way to the other side.

He apologised for being unable to play; his sense of duty had always been keen. Aged 40, so really rather old to be in battle, he was severely wounded and taken prisoner on 1 December 1917 at Honnechy, dying of his injuries the following day. The sadness of it all is summed up in this simple statement by Alfred le Maitre, looking back in 1930:

My particular hero was Blair in College. P.C.B. Blair, Head of School, and, what was more important, my fag master, was I think the kindest person that I ever knew. He was somewhere in the fifteen stones, and could discourse in the Greek and Latin of the polished pre-war civilisation. He was a cadet officer with sword (which I cleaned once), and after his Blue and International and great classical deeds at Cambridge, was killed.

The 1913 cricket XI; Alfred le Maitre is on the far left in the back row. He was severely wounded in the war. Next to him is the prizewinning Stephen Williamson, killed at Neuve Chapelle, aged 18.

Bibliography

Those with an interest in learning more about Fettes College will find its full history covered by Robert Philp's excellent *A Keen Wind Blows* (1998) and my own *Carrying On* (2012), both of which are available from the school shop (www.fettesshop.com). Alasdair Roberts' *Ties That Bind: Boys' Schools of Edinburgh* (2009) explores the history of the various institutions which competed – and indeed still compete – in the city's crowded academic market. Anthony Seldon and David Walsh have made an excellent contribution to this field with *Public Schools and the Great War* (2013), and I warmly recommend Trevor Royle's *The Flowers of the Forest: Scotland and the First World War* (2007).

W.B. Adam, *Naval Interlude* (MS, Fettes Archive, 1934-52)

Henry William Auden, *A Minimum of Greek* (Toronto, Morang & Co., 1906)

H.H. Austin, *With MacDonald in Africa* (London, Edward Arnold, 1903)

A.A.S. Barnes, *On Active Service with the Chinese Regiment* (London, Grant Richards, 1902)

Correlli Barnett, *Britain and Her Army, 1509–1970* (Allen Lane, 1970)

Winston Churchill, *The Story of the Malakand Field Force*, (London, 1897)

Saul David, *Zulu: the Heroism & Tragedy of the Zulu War of 1879* (London, Viking, 2004)

Clive Dewey, *Anglo-Indian Attitudes: the Mind of the Indian Civil Service* (London, Hambledon, 1993)

Rod Edmond, *Leprosy and Empire* (Cambridge, CUP, 2006)

Elie Parish Church Guild, *Rev. W.N. Monteith* (booklet, 2008)

Niall Ferguson, *The Pity of War* (London, Penguin, 1998)

Niall Ferguson, *Empire: How Britain made the Modern World* (London, Penguin, 2002)

A.I.R. Glasfurd, *Rifle and Romance in the Indian Jungle,* (London, John Lane, 1905)

Ian Hay, *Arms and the Men* (London, HMSO. 1950)

Howard Hensman, *A History Of Rhodesia* (Edinburgh, Blackwood, 1900)

Vernon Hesketh-Prichard, *Where Black Rules White* (New York, Charles Scribner, 1900)

Vernon Hesketh-Prichard, *Through the Heart of Patagonia* (New York, Appleton, 1902)

C.L.R. James, *Beyond a Boundary* (London, Hutchinson, 1963)

Denis Judd & Keith Surridge, *the Boer War* (Palgrave Macmillan, New York, 2003)

Robert Bruce Lockhart, *Memoirs of a British Agent* (London, Putnam, 1932)

Robert Bruce Lockhart, *Return to Malaya* (London, Putnam, 1936)

Robert Bruce Lockhart, *My Scottish Youth*, (London, Putnam, 1937)

Noel Loos, *White Christ, Black Cross: the emergence of a Black Church* (Canberra, Aboriginal Studies Press, 2007)

R.J. Mackenzie, *Almond of Loretto* (London, Constable, 1905)

Norman Macleod, *Fettes College Register* 6th Edition, (Edinburgh, Constable, 1932)

J.A. Mangan, *The Games Ethic and Imperialism* (London, Frank Cass, 1998)

J.A. Mangan, *Athleticism in the Victorian & Edwardian Public School* (London, Routledge, 2000)

W.K. McClure, *Italy in North Africa* (London, Constable, 1913)

C. Normand, *Normand Conquests*, (Family History)

Robert Philp, *A Keen Wind Blows: the story of Fettes College* (London, James & James, 1998)

Cecil Reddie, *Abbotsholme* (London, Allen, 1900)

Theodore Roosevelt, *The Rough Riders* (New York, Collier, 1899)

Edward Spiers, *Haldane – Army Reformer* (Edinburgh, University Press, 1980)

G. W. Steevens, *With Kitchener to Khartum* (New York, Dodd, Mead & Co., 1911)

Hew Strachan, *The Outbreak of the First World War* (Oxford, OUP, 2004)

Clive Whitehead, *Colonial Education* (London, I.B. Taurus, 2003)

Lewis Wroughton, *Colonial Reports – Annual, No. 710 Basutoland 1910-11* (London, HMSO, 1912)

The Author

David McDowell was educated at the Belfast Royal Academy and
Merton College, Oxford. He taught for twelve years at Collyer's
College, Horsham, before moving to Edinburgh in 2005. He
teaches History and Politics at Fettes.

David McDowell by Endel White of Horsham

Index

Notes

1 Karla Baker, 'Shady dealings in the whisky underworld', National Library of Scotland, 16 April 2010, http://blogs.nls.uk/bartholomew/?p=53 accesses 12 December 2013
2 Quoted in Robert Philp, *A Keen Wind Blows: the story of Fettes College* (London, James & James, 1998) p. i
3 C.L.R. James, *Beyond a Boundary* (London, Hutchinson, 1963) pp. 213-4
4 Kathryn Hughes, review of *High Minds: The Victorians and the Birth of Modern Britain*, by Simon Heffer, *The Guardian*, 29 November 2013
5 J.A. Mangan, *The Games Ethic and Imperialism* (London, Frank Cass, 1998) p. 18
6 EHD Sewell, *The Rugby Roll of Honour* (1919) quoted in Alastair McEwen, *Scottish Rugby International Casualties*, at Edinburgh's War (http://www.edinburghs-war.ed.ac.uk/sport/rugby) accessed 10/01/2014
7 Niall Ferguson, *Empire: How Britain made the Modern World* (London, Penguin, 2002), p. 260
8 C.L.R. James, op. cit, p. 32
9 R.J. Mackenzie, *Almond of Loretto* (London, Constable, 1905) p. 158
10 Quoted in J.A. Mangan (1998) p. 25
11 Quoted in J.A. Mangan, *Athleticism in the Victorian & Edwardian Public School* (London, Routledge, 2000) p. 110
12 W.K. McClure, *Italy in North Africa* (London, Constable, 1913) p. 242
13 Robert Bruce Lockhart, *Memoirs of a British Agent* (London, Putnam, 1932) p. 67
14 Ibid., p. 84
15 Ferguson, p. 261
16 C.L.R. James, p. 204
17 Lockhart (1936) p. 310
18 Norman Macleod, *Fettes College Register* 6th Edition, (Edinburgh, Constable, 1932) p. xxiii
19 Quoted in Philp, p. 17
20 Henry William Auden, *A Minimum of Greek* (Toronto, Morang & Co., 1906), p. 1
21 Ibid., p. 16
22 Cecil Reddie, *Abbotsholme* (London, Allen, 1900) p. 23
23 Philp, p. 24

[24] Archdeacon Averill, funeral oration for Charles Bowden, quoted in Christchurch City Libraries, *Upper Riccarton Cemetery*, Christchurch, 2007

[25] Quoted in Noel Loos, *White Christ, Black Cross: the emergence of a Black Church* (Canberra, Aboriginal Studies Press, 2007) p. 65

[26] Clive Dewey, *Anglo-Indian Attitudes: the Mind of the Indian Civil Service* (London, Hambledon, 1993) p. 3

[27] Jan Morris, p. 187

[28] Robert Bruce Lockhart, *My Scottish Youth*, (London, Putnam, 1937) p. 260

[29] Dewey, p. 6

[30] Quoted in *Black and White: A Weekly Illustrated Record and Review* (London) 22 January 1898

[31] 'Death of D.G. Campbell', Straits Times, 26 June 1918, at Singapore National Library Online Archive, http://eresources.nlb.gov.sg/newspapers/Digitised/Article/straitstimes19 180626-1.2.56.aspx, viewed 27 May 2014

[32] Clive Whitehead, *Colonial Education* (London, I.B. Taurus, 2003) p. 14

[33] Mangan (1998) p. 18

[34] Correlli Barnett, *Britain and Her Army, 1509–1970* (Allen Lane, 1970), p. 314

[35] Ian Hay, *Arms and the Men* (London, HMSO. 1950) p. 18

[36] Ibid., p. 25

[37] EHD Sewell in Alastair McEwen

[38] Quoted in ibid.

[39] Winston Churchill, *The Story of the Malakand Field Force*, (London, 1897) p.81

[40] Robert Bruce Lockhart, *Return to Malaya* (London, Putnam, 1936) p. 108

[41] Lockhart (1932) p. 13

[42] Clement Semmler, 'Ogilvie, William Henry (Will) (1869 - 1963)', *Australian Dictionary of Biography, Volume 11, (Melbourne, MUP, 1988) pp 70-71.*

[43] *Fettesian*, July 1893

[44] 'The Disaster to the SS Tararua', *Press*, 3 May 1881, at New Zealand National Library, http://paperspast.natlib.govt.nz/cgi-bin/paperspast?a=d&cl=search&d=CHP18810503.2.17&srpos=58&e= 01-04-1881-31-12-1882--100--1-byDA-on--0%22SS+Tararua%22-ARTICLE- accessed 12 December 2013

[45] Lewis Wroughton, *Colonial Reports – Annual, No. 710 Basutoland 1910-11*, London, HMSO, 1912 pp 11-12

[46] Zulu warrior Mehlokazulu, quoted in Saul David, *Zulu: the Heroism & Tragedy of the Zulu War of 1879* (London, Viking, 2004) p. 151

[47] G. W. Steevens, *With Kitchener to Khartum* (New York, Dodd, Mead & Co., 1911) p. 154

[48] See H.H. Austin, *With MacDonald in Africa* (London, Edward Arnold, 1903) pp. 42-9

[49] C. Normand, *Normand Conquests*, (Family History) p. 140

[50] Denis Judd & Keith Surridge, *the Boer War* (Palgrave Macmillan, New York, 2003) p. 55

[51] Rod Edmond, *Leprosy and Empire* (Cambridge, CUP, 2006) pp. 86-9

[52] Barnett, p. 353

[53] Mangan, p. 83

[54] H.W. Auden, 'Immigration of the West' *Daily Herald* (Calgary) 28th September 1903

[55] Lockhart (1936) p. 299

[56] A.I.R. Glasfurd, *Rifle and Romance in the Indian Jungle,* (London, John Lane, 1905) p. 4

[57] Another OF , Arthur Findlay, became a leading light in spiritualist circles and left his home, Stansted Hall, to become the national College for the Advancement of Psychic Science, which it still is.

[58] Theodore Roosevelt, *The Rough Riders* (New York, Collier, 1899) p. 177

[59] Henry Hamilton Fyfe, *The Illusion of National Character*, (London, 1940) p. 3

[60] A.A.S. Barnes, *On Active Service with the Chinese Regiment* (London, Grant Richards, 1902) p. 86

[61] Vernon Hesketh-Prichard, 'Haiti: Life in the First of the Negro Republics' in J.A. Hammerton (Ed.) *Peoples of All Nations* (London, Educational Book Co., 1920) p. 2559

[62] Vernon Hesketh-Prichard, *Where Black Rules White* (New York, Charles Scribner, 1900) p. 242

[63] Hesketh-Prichard (1900), pp. 281-4

[64] Vernon Hesketh-Prichard, *Through the Heart of Patagonia* (New York, Appleton, 1902) p. 298

[65] R.H. Heussler, quoted in Mangan (1998)., p. 112

[66] Hamilton Fyfe, p. 19

[67] Quoted in Elie Parish Church Guild, *Rev. W.N. Monteith* (booklet, 2008)

[68] McClure, p. 2

[69] Hew Strachan, *The Outbreak of the First World War* (Oxford, OUP,

2004) p. 177

[70] See Niall Ferguson, *The Pity of War* (London, Penguin, 1998) Ch.1

[71] Quoted in Edward Spiers, *Haldane – Army Reformer* (Edinburgh, University Press, 1980) p. 190

[72] Haldane, speech to Parliament, 13 May 1912, quoted in Spiers, p.141

[73] Strachan, p. 206

[74] Lockhart (1936), p. 301

Printed in Great Britain
by Amazon